Contents

I0467520

Version	Date	Revisions
1.0	9.30.15	Chapters 1 - 5
1.1	11.27.15	Chapters 6 - 8
1.2	12.20.15	Revisions

*Dedicated to my BB, my lil B, his lil b
and any other b's that may come to bless this b as they have.*

Preface

Shortly after the birth of my second son, I couldn't help but think that, in a weird way, he had it kind of easy. I knew he was tempting death with every unwashed touch and ill-fated sneeze. I was aware that his sensorial experience involved passing in and out of consciousness in various states of hunger, pain and fear. And I suspected that his nascent consciousness only allowed for what was essentially a Fisher-Price version of free will that, aside from bawling uncontrollably, generally consisted of the following three largely self-determined actions: a) vigorously track his surroundings with darting eyes and wildly unpredictable head movements, b) voraciously suck down all bottles and teats within a two inch spherical radius of his mouth and c) viciously pummel his diaper with an aural and viscous barrage while maintaining an admirably furrowed brow.

Now how could this semblance of a life possibly be construed as easy? The degrees of danger, discomfort and sheer confusion of those first few days out of the womb undoubtedly make for a trying time for all of us. However, even though those inaugural moments likely inflict trauma on most every human being as a first rite of passage, I would argue that there is a much more precarious state of existence to deal with today. Boredom.

From those first breaths to the moment we can sit ourselves down on our evolutionarily upright haunches and read this book, we have taken a long and often tumultuous journey towards earning a few precious moments of boredom. However, most of us do not see boredom as the just reward for resolutely grinding up a few microdegrees of free will in each passing moment of our waking lives. Most of us fear it.

You see, my son's state of existence was dreadful in a lot of ways. However, on the other hand, he also didn't have a lot of choices. Nor did he have a lot of skills and abilities at his disposal. He was quite literally starting with, in video game vernacular, zero experience points. So what may have been dreadful was also essentially inevitable in the short term. If my infant son were somehow suddenly able to attain an extraordinary level of self-awareness, he might have almost felt comforted in an "oh-well-is-what-it-is" kind of way.

The same cannot be said of most adult humans as much as we sometimes would like to convince ourselves otherwise. Almost every single one of us, if compared to those first harrowing days of existence, now has vastly more choices at our disposal.

And that is indeed terrifying.

For what to do with this hard-earned expanse of self-determination? Those of us who have had the good fortune of satisfying the elementary needs of food, clothing and shelter now have a much more difficult, much more existential conundrum on our hands. With the necessities out of the way, now what?

In the absence of a purpose born out of necessity, many of us have defaulted to more mundane objectives in life. In a lot of cases, we have just doubled down on material pursuits which have generally not made us any happier. In fact, a 2010 study by two Princeton researchers showed that, above $75k in annual income, the link between further wealth and a better emotional well-being breaks down (Deaton, 2010). Said another way, after a certain point, mo' money does not necessarily mean mo' happiness. So what to do?

When my wife and I were discharged from the hospital, they gave us an instruction pamphlet entitled "Mother and Newborn Education/Discharge Instructions". It was filled with helpful information on how not to screw up the precious life that you had just been bestowed. This pamphlet was presented as a series of basic principles on feeding, bathing, safety and, of course, pooping. Such guidance is vital to help shepherd our precious babies through those first moments and eventually on to more fruitful activities like picking their noses or borrowing our cars as teenagers.

The trouble is, none of us get such an instruction pamphlet when we become adults. Full of promise but lacking direction, we grown-ups fumble about and try to make sense of the wide open nature of life to varying degrees of success.

We have no "Education/Discharge Instructions for Becoming a Quality Person." Hypothetically, such a book would address two vital questions that each of us must necessarily face; "How do we find what will make us feel truly fulfilled?" and "How do we attain that once we find it?" Given that we are all individuals with distinct personalities and preferences, such a book could not be prescriptive in nature as no single prescription is a cure-all. However, it could perhaps find another way to be both broadly applicable and singularly relevant to each of us.

What we need is a universal touchstone for decision-making. However, rather than individually address the infinite range of decisions that face humanity, we need to deconstruct the nature of choice into its atomic parts. Much like all matter is constructed from the common building blocks of electrons and protons, what if all decisions had a similarly fundamental nature? If such a concept existed, surely it could help my two sons as they begin to make their own life decisions in incrementally more meaningful ways.

And that is why I chose to write this book. Through a series of inter-related essays, I wanted to explore some examples of well-known individuals and organizations that have successfully found a lasting purpose beyond the bare necessities. Whether a world-class sushi chef, a legendary golfer or a storied burger chain, these people and groups share two increasingly atypical traits; marked displays of excellence over a long period of time and deep-seated feelings of fulfillment that come with a sense of purpose. Indeed, they have filled those daunting moments of ennui with a fuller appreciation of life.

However, the goal of these essays is not to provide a how-to as to the specifics of each of their achievements. This is not a paint-by-numbers get-rich-quick book. Rather, it is the start of a conversation between myself and others as to the possible connections between excellence and purpose, between quality and fulfillment. By drawing upon the underlying principles common to the subjects of each of these essays, I hope to unearth a more universally effective framework for finding fulfillment, to unlock the afore-mentioned touchstone for decision-making. After all, if these people have found purpose while engaging in such a diverse array of activities then why can't the rest of us?

Thus, whether you are a dancer, a politician, a scientist, a welder, a priest or an oil magnate, the powerful frameworks within this book can serve as a guiding principle for you to lead a more rewarding, more fruitful and higher quality life. Furthermore, these concepts will also help to clarify some of the biggest misunderstandings of what makes humans uniquely happy and fulfilled.

Unlike our infant children who lack the luxury of choice, we as adults often reside ourselves to unfulfilling pursuits because we simply haven't come across any better options. The problem isn't how we progress but rather in what direction.

In that sense, the framework described in this book is not an endpoint but rather a rational starting point, an axiom if you will, for you to make your own decisions and find your own unique path. It is an Improvement Axiom for leading a higher quality life.

Part One:
Building the Axiom

While the Improvement Axiom is ultimately simple in construct, it does require a few building blocks, i.e. core principles that clarify some of the most fundamental misunderstandings in today's society. So through the course of Part One, we will establish these building blocks, leading up to a clear and simple mental map that we will refer to as the Improvement Axiom. This philosophical framework can be a tool, a compass to be more specific, to guide you past the noise of modern day life to what will uniquely make you as an individual feel truly fulfilled.

Chapter One:
The Secret of In-N-Out's Success

You never gain something but that you lose something.
- Henry David Thoreau

Here's an exercise just for fun. The next time you pass through a city in California, find some locals and ask them the following, "What is the best burger in California?" If you are a California local, or have lived there long enough to know the lay of the land, ask yourself the same question. No cheating.

I would venture a bet that a large percentage of your responses would point, not to some $22 foie gras topped concoction from some swanky Santa Monica establishment, but rather to a humble burger simply named the "Double Double" which can be had for something on the order of three dollars and fifty cents. In fact, ask any Californian expat which top 3 food establishments they miss most. I would venture a bet that most, if not all, respondents would have the birthplace of the Double Double on their list, i.e. In-N-Out.

Founded by a family of devout Christians in 1948, In-N-Out's focus on value, i.e. consistently high quality food at a reasonable price, has created a cultish following among west coasters. While other fast food menus have grown to increasingly unwieldy scales over the decades, In-N-Out's menu looks today almost exactly as it did in 1948. As in, they sell burgers, shakes and fries. That's it. The burgers themselves are simple to a fault as well. Lightly grilled bun, patty, lettuce, tomato, onions, cheese, special sauce. This combination of ingredients is grilled, toasted, stacked and wrapped so perfectly and so neatly millions of times a year at each of the company's 250+ locations that the company has incrementally built one of the most respected fast food brands in the world (In-N-Out Burger - Wikipedia, the free encyclopedia, 2015).

In-N-Out stands as one of the most exemplary models of "Keeping It Simple, Stupid". While this is certainly not the only way to drive towards a high quality result, it has worked wonders for In-N-Out and the founding family which continues to run it today.

And yet, we've glossed over something important here. What exactly does it mean to be consistently "high quality"? What is "quality" for that matter? Why the heck do so many people (including myself) reminisce so fondly about a humble burger from a single-mindedly simple restaurant establishment?

Is it the taste? Is it the consistency? Is it the fact that the price is less than $4? How can we know definitively that this burger is a high quality burger? Is this burger intrinsically tasty? Is its burger-ness approaching some platonic ideal of burger-dom? Or is there something else going on here that is more universal? Is there something we can extract from the example of In-N-Out that could meaningfully improve our own lives? Answer this and we will have the first building block of the Improvement Axiom.

To start to tackle the question of what is quality, imagine you are walking down a crowded street and see two people staring intently at something just above and over your left shoulder. What would you do? You probably tilted your head to the side and looked with them, if only for a brief moment. If the object of focus was particularly interesting, you may have lingered even longer. In fact, if you stood there long enough and the foot traffic on that particular path active enough, you may have looked down to find yourself not standing next to two people but standing in a crowd, all looking intently at the same thing.

In our caveman days, this instinct likely served a very critical purpose. If you were munching on a T-bone and noticed three of your prehistoric brethren suddenly turn and face the same direction, you had two choices: a) continue to enjoy your steak bone or b) look in that direction as well. If you chose "Option A", then depending on your luck and environmental surroundings, you may have aptly chosen to continue dinner and ignore your pals. Or, you may have just missed something very important. A particularly fetching cavewoman for instance. Or a hungry saber-toothed tiger. As such, from an evolutionary perspective, there's good reason why we have an ingrained need to peak where others look.

So in the context of quality, it's understandable that, to a large extent, our default rule of thumb for finding high quality things is to look where others are looking. While the means with which this dynamic takes place has dramatically changed since 20,000 B.C., the underlying mechanics of why it happens is very much the same. Prior to the internet, our eyes were drawn towards the focal point of others eyeballs and our ears were perked by effusive word of mouth. Today, our eyes are drawn towards the digital focal point of others in the form of "likes", "re-tweets" and forwards. Our ears are drawn to the steady barrage of aural advertisements emanating from tv, radio and now, streaming internet.

In either case, we generally look because we don't want to miss something important. It could be important as in dangerous. Or it could be important-beautiful. Or important-puzzling. Or important-mind-blowing. The problem is, this barrage has shown no sign of slowing down. And as the bombardment intensifies over time, we find ourselves in an arms race of "likes", where only the peak outliers that exhibit asymptotic growth can survive our filters for attention and mind share.

And so, whereas in the caveman days the determination of what was important or not was made around a campfire or a roasting spit with some primordial deer carcass, in our modern day, this determination is made on a global scale, traveling at the speed of light through the air and space, and made through a medium of emoticons, tweets, posts, reposts and likes. It is the wisdom of crowds on steroids and it is the current in which modern existence swims and by which modern society, to a larger and larger extent, tries to determine what is high quality and what is not.

But here's the rub. How do you know the crowd is really all that... wise? And is the crowd wiser on certain topics than others? For instance, the crowd that likes In-N-Out is vast enough and dogged enough in their appreciation for the humble Double Double that you would almost be foolish to write it off as simply bad taste on a mass scale. But does the same go for say... the crowd that loves Keep Up With the Kardashians? Or the crowd that loves the Chicago Bulls? Or, dare I say it, the GOP?

Which one of these crowds is most likely to correctly determine what is high quality vs low quality? Without a proper framework to make this decision for ourselves on an individual basis, I would argue that we find ourselves, not only dependent on the wisdom of the crowds, but beholden to them. Without an objective framework to define quality in our own minds, we default to the judgment of crowds as a stand-in for our own belief system and preferences. What is worse, in the age of the "swipe-right" internet, it is easier than ever to find a crowd that at least demographically looks and thinks like you. The In-N-Out eating, Kardashian-watching, GOP crowd if you will. And, as a result, it is easier than ever to adopt the doctrine that your crowd is way more informed, articulate and savvy than say the In-N-Out eating, Kardashian-watching, Libertarian folk regardless as to whether this is actually grounded in any sort of facts. This is also known as groupthink and it's a problem.

So how do we address this natural tendency towards groupthink? I believe there is an answer. And it's not my answer. To this we look to Robert Pirsig's *Zen and the Art of Motorcycle Maintenance*.

The Double Double is a Fiber Optic

When I first came across Robert Pirsig's *Zen and the Art of Motorcycle Maintenance*, I didn't know quite what to expect. Perusing Amazon reviews led me to believe that this was an interesting book on philosophy with a handyman twist but not necessarily a tour de force. I was wrong. Robert Pirsig's book is the most important philosophical work in recent collective memory.

And the reason for that is this; there is one critical fallacy at an individual and societal level that plagues our world today; the belief that quality is intrinsic and inherent in a thing, i.e. something that can be measured, like height, weight or pH level. Hard to believe at first, but this is the root cause of so many contemporary ills: patient zero. Pirsig understood this and attempted to dismantle and reverse this misunderstanding through the course of "Zen".

While I won't make an ill-fated effort to plagiarize Pirsig's logic in reaching his conclusion (that you would be best served to read for yourself), I will attempt to paraphrase his most critical finding as it serves as one crucial leg of the Improvement Axiom. This finding involves our fundamental understanding, or rather misunderstanding, of the concept of Quality (which Pirsig denotes with a capital "Q" to highlight its importance).

In recalling a cross-country motorcycle trip between an estranged father and son, Pirsig's work is largely autobiographical. The father, who serves as the narrator of the novel, reflects on his past life as a troubled teacher at a small college. Through the course of the book, the narrator becomes obsessed with defining the concept of Quality which he believes to be inherently undefinable, a frustratingly irreconcilable paradox.

It is the undefinable nature of Quality that the narrator, and, in turn, Pirsig, believes is the root of some of modern society's most misguided pursuits. Similar to our prior example of the humble Double Double, the trouble, Pirsig poses, is that the modern scientific method is obsessed with measurement and observation at the specific exclusion of any form of subjectivity. While this has worked for innumerable scientific discoveries to date and is credited with progression of society from the Industrial Revolution through the Internet era, Pirsig argues we are beginning to reach diminishing returns from science's ability to improve our well-being despite what seems like an acceleration of technological advances year after year.

The problem is, even as we build faster, stronger, smarter things, we have still never been sure whether we are actually building **better** things. The scientific method assumes all things can be objectively measured and therefore understood. Quality, an inherently subjective and personal concept, defies this assumption and thus forever evades the grasp of the scientific method. But that doesn't stop science from trying.

The economic motivations for trying is relatively rational. Imagine, if you will, you had a little black box that automatically understood and calculated the quality of something and told you, in discrete numerical terms, how to replicate it. A recipe if you will. Imagine this formula could be universally applied to all things, from rock bands to politics to crème brulee. Whoever owned this little black box would, not wholly fantastical, probably rule the world. In the history of mankind, Google's PageRank algorithm has probably come closest to replicating this "black box". And we've seen how well it's done for them. And yet, even so, now that we have the power of search at our finger tips, the definition of quality still remains elusive. Is it a string or a particle? Or are we not even asking the right questions?

A question like, for example, how do you truly measure "quality"? Revisiting the Double Double, we know it's a good quality burger, but how do we measure this "burger-ness" in discrete "burgometers™"? As absurd as this question sounds, billions of dollars a year are shoveled into consumer research to try to answer questions just like this. In fact, $6.7bn are spent every year in the United States alone on this exact type of marketing research (Anderson, 2010). Year after year, time, effort and capital are thrown at unlocking the mysteries of quality. And they are completely missing the point.

Study after study focuses on the symptoms but rarely the cause. Statistical analyses break down demographic preferences. Marketing consultants do countless surveys on customer feedback. While this work can help point someone in the right direction, they often miss the forest through the trees.

Again, let's take the Double Double. I am sure studies have attempted to tie the Double Double's ingredients, salt content, umami and freshness levels et al with the concept of "quality" in the hopes that by duplicating those various discrete metrics, they could in effect recreate the singular success of In-N-Out, the "black box" recipe if you will. And they are ultimately doomed to failure. Don't get me wrong, some may get close to scientifically and methodically recreating a single In-N-Out burger[1], but there will never be a perfect replication of its success as a whole.

Pirsig's central thesis can shed some light on why this is so; Quality is not a singular trait to be measured by an observer. It is not a "thing" to be observed. It is the act of observing itself. Or experiencing. Or feeling. Or tasting. Quality exists in the relationship between two things. It exists between an actor and his audience. Between a scientist and his subject. And, yes, even between a hungry human and his burger. Quality exists *between* the observer and the observed not *within* either party.

Consider for a moment the most broadly accepted measures of quality presently, i.e. user-defined ratings (e.g. four stars, likes, percentiles, thumbs ups, etc.) on books, restaurants, movies, employers, etc. What do all of these ratings have in common? They are helpful as an aggregate of personal sentiments and interactions. However, what they offer in summation they lack in specificity.

On a granular level, these rating systems only speak to a vaguely positive or negative sentiment that each reviewer has had in interacting with said product, firm or service. Beyond that, the usefulness of these metrics as a tool to tease out broadly applicable characteristics of quality breaks down very quickly.

---

[1] Kudos to J. Kenji Lopez-Alt (http://www.kenjilopezalt.com/) and his masterful reverse engineering of the Double Double. Try it for yourself! Search for "In-N-Out double-double recipe" at www.seriouseats.com

For example, one can measure the reliability and suction of a vacuum cleaner, but how does that measure apply to movies? Sounds like a silly question but correlating any rating across mediums will lead to nonsensical comparisons of this sort. Furthermore, each individual will find different characteristics attractive or repulsive. Another individual may find the exact inverse relationship true. Thus, even our most reliable measure of quality to date is inherently flawed, providing broad indicators of positivity or negativity but never providing lasting insight into the common factors that generate these personal impressions.

This is because quality cannot be measured in such a quantitative manner. It can be informed by these metrics, but since personal sentiment about any given experience is just that, personal, then ultimately any measure of quality that is based on outwardly measurable traits will fall short of pinpointing the precise recipe of the "black box."

Although this observation may seem a bit deflating at first, it is in fact essential for opening ourselves to a broader understanding of what quality is. It is for this reason that, without hyperbole but perhaps with a degree of irony, Robert Pirsig's scientifically rational conclusion on the limits of scientific measures is his lasting gift to mankind. (Pirsig, 1974, 1999)

If this is true, if quality is in fact not inherent to an object but rather in the eye of the beholder, then how can we ever hope to understand it? Shouldn't then the concept of big "Q" Quality be as varied and innumerous as there are observers in the world? Well, yes, actually. But the fact that, even with this diversity of opinion, a legion of people still found a common love in In-N-Out shows that there is perhaps a deeper, more universal, relationship at play here. As hinted earlier, the success of In-N-Out is rooted in the singular focus of its founding family to creating consistently fresh and delicious burgers at a reasonable price. All the work they put in to maintain this as a collective organization is felt by its customers. So can you see what drives the quality relationship in this case? Can you guess which parties are on either end of the two tin cans and a string?

Rather than rely on outward measures, let's start with the symptom and pinch-zoom out, CSI style. The Double Double is tasty, yes, but if you take one step back from the burger, you see that its tastiness was a result of the care with which the employee cooked the burger and prepared it. You take a step back from that and you see that great care was taken to train the employee and maintain a culture of excellence. Zoom out further, and you see this great care extends to the organization's very supply chain which delivers fresh ingredients directly from two plants in Texas and California without ever being frozen, geographically limiting its own expansion to ensure that this vital piece of quality control stays intact. You take a step back from that and you see that it is the guiding principle of the original founders and their focus on quality, value and consistency above all else (including revenue growth and global fast food domination) that drives each of these actions from macro to micro to your mouth.

Ultimately, if you agree that quality is defined as a relationship rather than an inherent trait, what does this mean? That it takes everyone from the Founders to the meat suppliers, to the truck drivers, to the managers, and finally down to the line cook focused on producing a quality result, being "in the zone" if you will, to ensure that you consistently experience a quality result. No easy task. From the individual up to the organization, they are just cooking burgers in some sense, but in another they are using the burger to satisfy, nay, to communicate with their customers the following: "You matter. You are worth the effort. And you deserve this awesome burger. Enjoy."

You deserve this awesome burger... You don't need to see this mission statement written down to know that it is true. You feel it, you taste it, it resonates within you. The burger, as they say, speaks for itself. This is a product of a high quality relationship, an effect. While there are a lot of potential causes for this effect, the most critical driver for In-N-Out's quality is a deep-felt empathy and concern for its customers. As an organization, In-N-Out sustains this level of empathy across its entire employee base exceptionally well, transmitting it from the Founders on down to the line cooks. The last leg of this vital transmission is through its food. In this way, the Double Double is like a fiber optic connecting In-N-Out with its customers. The message it carries is strong and consistent. Go to any of their 300 restaurants and you will find this connection expertly and meticulously maintained.

This deep-felt empathy and concern is core to high quality signals, it shrinks the distance between the sender and the receiver. The medium In-N-Out chose, in this case a burger, was one they were uniquely passionate and knowledgeable about. Nonetheless, it is worth noting that the diversity of mediums available is as broad as the people who master them. Whether "you deserve" an inspiring ballet performance, a stirring oratory, a ground-breaking scientific discovery, a solid steel foundation, a heartfelt sermon or an expertly-refined petroleum, the message contained within any truly high quality relationship is ultimately very similar: "I want to share this with you because you matter." But the diversity of mediums also matters. It is the spice of life. And that is what truly makes a Double Double so delicious.

Quality is a relationship. Like placing a piece in a puzzle, this concept unlocks the next building block of the Improvement Axiom. Let's explore how. If quality is a relationship rather than an inherent thing, it tells us that every time you come across something high quality that was man-made, whether a food, a work of art, or an event, etc., then some person or persons has sent a message that you have received. They put their creation into the world and you picked up on it, like a receiver to a radio tower. Now this is where it gets very interesting. For every signal, there is a source, find something high quality and you will always find a high quality source behind it.

If there is always a high quality source, then this, in turn, tells you two things. First, with enough research, it is possible to learn how that source managed to send such a clear message of quality, how that single radio tower worked. Second, over time, it must be possible to do this across vastly different mediums in hopes of finding a common thread, a universal frequency being used. If there was, this would be the aforementioned black box. And there is. The black box exists. And one can be found in a subway station in Tokyo.

Chapter One Thought Exercises

Quality is a Relationship.

Try to think of things that you have come across that you feel are high quality. It could be a conversation, a book, a meal, an app, even a unique piece of furniture. What about that interaction resonates with you? What message do you think is being communicated to you through it? Who is sending the message?

Explore this concept of Quality as a Relationship in your own life. Don't just default to outward metrics. Instead, explore what kind of relationship the source of that interaction is trying to establish with you.

Chapter Two:
A Lesson From Jiro

I do the same thing over and over, improving bit by bit.
- Jiro Ono

In 2011, a documentary filmed by David Gelb came out that seemed to catch the imagination of the public, including mine. It was called *Jiro Dreams of Sushi* and it tracked the life of 85-year-old sushi master, Jiro Ono, and how, over a lifetime of daily routine, like a single stream of water etching a hole in stone, Jiro has etched out one of the finest sushi experiences in the world. On the surface, the quality of Jiro's work is almost self-evident. Three Michelin stars. President Obama and Shinzo Abe dining there in 2014. Countless celebrities making it a point to visit his 10-seat restaurant. A month long wait list that fills the moment it becomes available. Yes, this is damn good sushi. Arguably the best in the world as pronounced by some who claim to know a thing or two about food, including fellow Michelin chef Joel Robuchon.

This is Jiro's radio tower. It took 85 years to build, but it's signal strength has never been stronger and more pronounced. But, even so, let's not rely on the crowds, no matter who they are or what countries they happen to be running right now. Let's dig deeper.

There must be something here to tell us what makes Jiro's signal so strong, and his frequency so penetrating. An astute observation by the late Roger Ebert gives us an insightful glimpse into this mystery, a "portrait of tunnel vision" as he refers to it:

> "While watching it, I found myself drawn into the mystery of this man. Are there any unrealized wishes in his life? Secret diversions? Regrets? If you find an occupation you love and spend your entire life working at it, is that enough?
>
> Standing behind his counter, Jiro notices things. Some customers are left-handed, some right-handed. That helps determine where they are seated at his counter. As he serves a perfect piece of sushi, he observes it being eaten. He knows the history of that piece of seafood. He knows his staff has recently started massaging an octopus for 45 minutes and not half an hour, for example. Does he search a customer's eyes for a signal that this change has been an improvement? Half an hour of massage was good enough to win three Michelin stars. You realize the tragedy of Jiro Ono's life is that there are not, and will never be, four stars." (Ebert, 2012)

There is a reason I believe this documentary caught the imagination of the public when it was released. Like Jiro, it's subject was incredibly focused. It was incredibly timely. And it spoke to a deep and growing but almost unobservable cynicism that we as a society have developed in the face of the cacophony of crowds. Here was a man who's only obsession is not money, not power, not fame, but the perfect piece of sushi. If he had listened to the prevalent wisdom of the crowds, he may have picked a very different path, or at the very least, created a world-dominating chain of sushi franchises, like Colonel Sanders before him.

But Jiro's path is not a well-trodden one, it is a relentless pursuit of quality. In narrowing his focus, like a lens directing sunlight to a single focal point, Jiro has increased his signal-to-noise ratio to other-worldly levels. And in that, he has demonstrated the immense power of the concept of quality as a relationship.

Take a look again at Roger Ebert's description. Jiro notices things, whether customers are left or right handed. He serves. He observes. He knows the history of the food but he constantly seeks more. He makes a change to how he prepares. He searches his customer's eyes for a signal that this change has been an improvement. The signal. These are the signs of a master tuning his frequency. This is the black box.

Observation

One sign of a high quality source is an astute power of observation. Observation is essential for the tuning process. Without a process in place to receive feedback, a radio tower only sends a signal one direction. Over time, a radio tower that only sends a signal out but never receives a response back may find itself broadcasting on a frequency that no one is tuned into. This does not result in a very strong signal no matter how positive its content.

With all the little observations Jiro makes, from noticing which hand a customer favors, to watching the signals in their eyes as they eat is one critical component of the black box. In contrast to the mass marketing surveys mentioned in Chapter One, this is not an impersonal check-the-box questionnaire. This is communication at a very deep level.

Jiro doesn't talk very much in the documentary and probably talks even less in real life. But he is always communicating. The give and take between him and his customers is the life blood that keeps him going, keeps him tuned to his relentless pursuit and gives an endless stream of feedback that he can continue to use ad infinitum. He doesn't speak, but, like a stand-up comedian testing a different delivery of the same material, his decision to massage the octopus another 15 minutes is almost methodically experimental. It is, in fact, very similar to the tuning of a radio transistor. And he is checking if the signal lands more clearly.

Knowledge

To say the least, sushi has a long history in Japan. To be arguably the best sushi master in Tokyo is akin to being unanimously acknowledged as the best programmer in Silicon Valley. To be recognized as such in an area, geographically and professionally, so saturated with brilliance is in itself amazing. But, similar to how programming is built upon the logical foundations and discoveries of those who came before, so it is with sushi, and really any pursuit of quality. The feedback loop isn't just relevant for customers. It is relevant for history. You see, quality is a funny thing, it has no upper limit. This is pretty awesome especially if you like sushi. However, the other funny thing about quality is that the higher you go, it's like approaching the exosphere of Earth's atmosphere, it gets really really hard to push that much higher still.

The reason for this is that, like space exploration, as you push the limits of quality, you inevitably come across thresholds that have previously never been surpassed by humanity. It is quite literally, an undiscovered country. As such, there's a couple ways a particularly focused explorer could go. Build upon what has been discovered before and try to push it further than anyone else has before. Or, assume everything else that has come before is now bunk and try something completely different. Neither option is wrong per se. The first requires extreme mastery of what came before, i.e. depth of knowledge. The second requires understanding of what came before and extreme mastery of a broader range of previously unconnected mediums, i.e. breadth of knowledge. But without an ounce of doubt, success in either strategy, requires knowledge of what came before. Building on it or disregarding it are then up to you.

Jiro is an extreme example of the first strategy. He mastered the skill of sushi preparation in a historical context, understanding not only the how, but the why of long standing sushi secrets. And then he began his lifelong effort to further atomize those reasons, reverse engineering, deconstructing and reconstructing each ingredient and each process.

The second strategy is even more interesting and is perhaps best exemplified by Olympian high jumper Dick Fosbury. Prior to 1965, most world-class high jumpers used a variety of techniques that all ended with the jumper landing on their feet to prevent injury. However, as the sport transitioned to deeper foam mats, an opportunity arose.

In part due to fortuitous timing but more so a result of mindful experimentation, Dick Fosbury happened to develop a technique through trial and error that took advantage of this change in the sport. With thick mats, prior assumptions no longer held. So Fosbury did away with those techniques which were previously sacrosanct.

"Who lands on their back?!" the experts cried. But protests quickly subsided once Fosbury established a new world record at the '68 Olympics in Mexico City. The Fosbury Flop as it has come to be known has since become the only technique used by world-class high jumpers. (Fosbury Flop - Wikipedia, the free encyclopedia, 2015)

In either Jiro or Fosbury's case, there was a deep knowledge, and typically mastery, of the techniques that came before. Picasso didn't start as a Cubist, he started by mastering the techniques of the old masters, then he redirected those skills in a completely different direction. To send a quality signal, you could start with a blank slate, but it will take you a lot longer. Why not save the time and learn what the masters have done before you and why? Then you can decide what to take and what to leave behind. This is another component of the black box.

Iteration

The final piece of the black box is of the most philosophical importance. Iteration, which is typical to any process of tuning, is critical to forming a quality signal over time. Jiro, Fosbury, Picasso and others all use iteration in a never-ending loop of trial and error to improve their crafts. At first, this iteration resembles practice, as the initial skillsets are molded and perfected. Then, as the so-called ten thousand hours of practice evolves to mastery, iteration takes on another purpose: discovery and experimentation.

But there is something else significant about this process. Can you think of another field that similarly iterates in such a methodical manner? In an almost... scientifically methodical manner? Yes, modern science is built upon this process of iteration, of carefully testing and observing feedback. As mentioned in chapter one, this is the root of the scientific method to the specific exclusion of any form of subjectivity which, to date, have been typically attributed to the "arts". But could it be that there is more of a connection between the "arts" and "sciences" than we had previously thought? It is not hard to imagine that, in another lifetime, Jiro could have been an equally effective scientist, single-mindedly driving towards ground-breaking discoveries.

So why does there seem to be an ever widening chasm between what is deemed "art" and what is deemed "science"? Science seems to believe that art is too "subjective", too willy nilly, too freeform to be of real value to progressing the human mind. In a fitting tit for tat, Art seems to believe that science is too "objective", too cold, too rational to be of real value to progressing the human spirit. As our daily lives become more engrossed by the products of science, this widening chasm has very real implications.

The commonality of iteration provides a crucial clue as to how we can finally bridge this divide. Jiro, Fosbury, Picasso and other masters of arts do exhibit this very scientific trait without a doubt. So why don't we find more scientists that are able to cross the divide and make a comparably heartfelt impact on our psyches? Why can't we pick up their signal in the same way?

Intent

If the arts can be more methodical in their discovery process, then the sciences can be more empathetic to their audience. Methodical iteration in a vacuum **is** cold. But methodical iteration with the intent to connect with others is not. If science were to make this leap more often we would have a better idea as to whether simply making something faster, stronger or smarter for the sake of doing so is really **better**. Thus, understanding our own intent is critical to the iteration process.

In the same way In-N-Out essentially has "you deserve this awesome burger" as a powerful intent behind all that it does, Jiro turns this sense of purpose up to eleven by sending the following signal: "I will not rest until I deliver to you the most perfect piece of sushi on the planet". Both intents are admirably focused on a positive message, but you can see how Jiro has taken even In-N-Out's focus to a whole other level. Without these focal points, even Jiro and In-N-Out would have found it difficult to contain the inevitable entropy induced by constant iteration.

So in exploring the process of a humble sushi chef, we've come across our second building block of the Improvement Axiom, the common thread between high quality sources, the eponymous "black box". A peak inside the "black box" of quality reveals that there are common traits of observation, knowledge and iteration shared by high quality sources and a thread of positive intent that sews these traits together into a powerful signal. Interestingly, understanding and identifying this positive intent may help modern science finally resolve its quantum conundrum of quality. You may not be able to measure burgometers™ in real life, but you can measure the performance and reputation of organizations over time that demonstrate the three aforementioned common traits in addition to a strong positive intent.

While this may be an effective way to track the Fortune 500, it doesn't necessarily help shed light on those who spend their time on more solitary pursuits. So far, we have two building blocks for the Improvement Axiom: Quality as a Relationship and the Black Box. Both of these building blocks are relatively easy to ascribe to scenarios where there are clear relationships between two parties. A burger maker and a burger eater. Or a sushi maker and a sushi eater. Or a review writer and a review reader. A documentary filmmaker- you get the idea.

But what about Fosbury? Not only an oddity in the world of world-class high jumping, he poses some interesting questions about the two legs of the Improvement Axiom established thus far as well. Who the heck was his quality relationship established with? For this, we look to the third building block of the Improvement Axiom and one of the most solitary and mysterious pursuits of all: golf.

Chapter Two Thought Exercises

The Black Box.

Recall the things you observed as being high quality in Chapter One. Think of the source that you determined was sending you the high quality signal. Does that source exhibit traits of the black box? What is its feedback loop? How does it iterate? Could you do the same?

Consider a skill or craft you would like to improve in your own life. Explore different measures of feedback that you may be able to observe for that craft. Keep track of this feedback and experiment over time to improve the strength and positivity of the signal. Tune your own radio tower.

Chapter Three:
Zen and the Art of the Perfect Golf Swing

The only thing a golfer needs is more daylight.
- Ben Hogan

There is a famous golf photo of golf legend Ben Hogan (hint: search for "Ben Hogan 1 iron") that captures him staring down the fairway on the 18th hole in the final round of the 1950 US Open at Merion, holding his signature follow-through and framed by crowds of onlookers all the way down to the green in the distance. The photo itself is beautiful, but there are a few things about it that are particularly remarkable. The first is that he is perfectly striking a 1-iron which, as Lee Trevino once pointed out, "even God can't hit a 1-iron." The second is that this photo happens to capture, at moment of impact, an improbable shot during an equally improbable comeback and victory. The final and most remarkable thing about this photo is that it was taken just sixteen months after a near fatal car crash almost ended Hogan's legendary golf career. It's no mystery then why this photo and the story around it have been forever immortalized in golf lore as the "Miracle at Merion".

However, the moment captured by this photo was not created out of thin air. Like Jiro's sushi, it was finely crafted. All the initial components of the black box are there: observation, knowledge and iteration. Hogan was revered for his level of astute introspection and his ability to self-diagnose his own swing mechanics over years of practice. He was also infamous for the grueling nature of his practice regime through which this fine tuning took place. And finally, as much a student of the game as a master of it, Hogan attributed much of what he learned to those around him starting with the young golfer he caddied for when he first picked up the game. So what about his positive intent?

Ben Hogan was known to be more than somewhat elusive. Even the photographer who captured that famous photo, known as a master of photography in his own right, described Hogan as follows.

> *"Hogan was a mystery to me. But I didn't think about it. He was distant. You shot pictures of him, he was (in the) distance. Sammy Snead – friendly. Ben Hogan – distant."* (Posnanski, 2013)

So if Hogan didn't seem particularly interested in the opinion or reaction of others, who or what was he broadcasting his signal to? For that matter, what does any golfer get out of this singularly solitary sport? Very few of us have the US Open as a stage for our golf game. Even fewer of us even have the hopes of ever emulating a single one of Hogan's shots. And yet, millions of golfers make their way to the greens, entranced by the siren song of golf. This is all in the name of improving their game, or, more specifically, pursuing a high quality swing.

If I were to use my own golf game as a case study, the fewer people who could witness it the better, frankly. Nevertheless, despite the sad state of my golf game, or absence thereof to be more accurate, I, too, find myself drawn to the practice range to try to experience that perfect shot. And every once in a while when I do hit that one shot, I don't need a gallery of onlookers to tell me that it was the one. The quality of the shot itself reverberates and you feel the impact vibrate up your arms as you see the flight path of the ball trail into the distance, straight as an arrow. In lieu of this, a suspiciously Zen-like question arises; if a golfer hits a perfect shot and no one is there to witness it, was a signal ever sent?

The answer to this Zen-like riddle will unlock the third building block of the Improvement Axiom. To shed some light on the answer, who best to speak to it than Ben Hogan himself? In a revealing interview published by *Golf Magazine* in 1987, Hogan was asked whom he competed against: himself, the golf course or the rest of the field? This was his answer:

> *"All three. First I went after the golf course. Generally, I figured that if I could beat the course I could stay ahead of the competition. Ultimately, however, I guess I played against my own standards. It was a constant struggle of one kind or another—but always a pleasant one." (Peper, 1987)*

This is not only a succinct description of the challenge of golf but also of any other sport or activity where competition is involved. Competition is feedback. To compete is to put yourself against an opposing force, whether that is a force of nature, a field of competitors or, more often than not, yourself. Hogan understood that it was the constant struggle that allowed him to improve. Without it, he would have had no mechanism to judge his own growth.

However, the struggle of competition in itself isn't necessarily a positive signal or intent. It can, in a lot of cases, be particularly grueling, even unpleasant if the circumstances are not healthy. So how do we parse out the positive attributes of competition? Where is the positive intent in competition? The key is in Hogan's description of the constant struggle, it took on many forms, but it was always... pleasant?

The usage of the word pleasant seems like almost a throwaway at first, a way for Hogan to downplay his own extreme competitiveness. However, I believe there is another level to Hogan's description. It may be hard to imagine competition as being anything resembling pleasant. The definition of competition is to put oneself outside of one's comfort zone, to find an equal and opposing force to throw oneself at in hopes of getting some feedback as to one's growth. So how in the world can this be pleasant? A do-or-die drive in the closing seconds of the Super Bowl is stomach-churning, yes, terrifying, yes, nauseating, probably, but pleasant? Like smelling flowers on a crisp spring morning pleasant? Heavens no. Thankfully, Hogan once again can shed some light on this.

> *"You hear stories about me beating my brains out practicing, but the truth is, I was enjoying myself. I couldn't wait to get up in the morning so I could hit balls. I'd be at the practice tee at the crack of dawn, hit balls for a few hours, then take a break and get right back to it. And I still thoroughly enjoy it. When I'm hitting the ball where I want, hard and crisply—*

when anyone is—it's a joy that very few people experience."
(Peper, 1987)

In truth, Hogan described it as pleasant because he truly felt that it was. He was enjoying himself! His joy was deeper than just enjoying a mint julep on the porch of the clubhouse. This is the deep-felt joy of pursuing high quality, indeed, a joy "that very few people experience". When he hits the ball where he wants, he describes it as *hard* and *crisp*. You can almost imagine how it feels, the vibration through the arms, the instant positive feedback. Some call this being "in the zone". For those that have experienced being "in the zone" in any context, you know the feeling when you are fully in the moment. You are neither fully in control nor fully at the whim of your environment. You lose track of time. You are a tuning fork that has been struck and your frequency is in tune with everything around you. This is the feeling of absolute engagement in the pursuit of quality.

In this way, the pursuit of quality is itself its own reward. When this harmonious type of feedback is received, whether from the satisfied twinkle in a customer's eye or the vibration of a perfect golf impact or the flow of a basketball arc as it drops effortlessly through the net... swish, that is the joy that makes life more deeply rewarding.

However, as Hogan implied in his responses, this joy is not given, it is earned. It accumulates only after persistent focus and an absolute engagement in discovering the minutiae that make up a quality signal. The tuning process, the persistent iteration, is what generates the little vibrations. When you keep working at something, trying to understand it, to improve it, to solve it and then finally- it clicks. It's these little tremors of positive feedback, in turn, that keep you going, keep you iterating further to reach new heights. It can be a beautifully virtuous cycle. Even better, you don't necessarily need an audience to enjoy it. If quality is a relationship between two things, why can't those two things be the same thing? The answer, it can be.

Relationships exist all around us, if you thought about all the possible permutations of relationships between any two things, you would probably drive yourself mad (and in fact, Robert Pirsig, like the narrator in his novel, was institutionalized a number of times between 1961 and 1963). So how do we make sense of it?

Imagine a relationship is a string between two points which, when plucked, generates a certain frequency. When the line cook at In-N-Out grills a customer's patty in just the right way, a line is plucked and a positive frequency generated. When Jiro finds a tweak to his sushi preparation that further improves its texture, a line is plucked and a tremor is felt. When Dick Fosbury cleared a bar that no one had ever jumped in a way no one had ever imagined, a string inside his heart was plucked and a tremor was sent forth through the world. And when Ben Hogan struck the ball with his 1-iron on the 18th hole at Merion, not only did he receive the feedback in his heart, he felt a literal vibration in his arm just as the crowd felt a tremor of suspense in their bellies and a master photographer clicked his shutter, anticipating something historic wavering in the air.

There are some moments in history where a series of small vibrations, built up over years and years, layered one over the other, some low frequency, strung low and deep across time, some sharp and high, punctuating a precise point in time, come together in sync at the exact right moment, so much so that they create a harmony that is so strong, so distinct and so positive that it quite literally reverberates through time thereafter. Ben Hogan's strike was one of those moments. Harmonious.

We are not all Ben Hogan, this is true. But the beauty of seeking quality is that time spent alone, generating those small rhythms and melodies, is not wasted. Like a master chef who works tirelessly in her kitchen to discover a new ground-breaking dish, all those who pursue quality share this feeling on some level. To be true, if the Black Box is the recipe for quality, then this Sense of Resonance is the "joy of cooking".

This internal sensation of resonance is the third building block of the Improvement Axiom and completes our exploration of the concept of Quality. However, there is one more crucial factor beyond even quality that we must explore. This factor has come to be nearly synonymous with the subject of our next chapter, i.e. the most valuable enterprise the world has ever seen. Apple.

Chapter Three Thought Exercises

Sense of Resonance.

Recall any time you lost yourself in an activity, any activity. How did it feel? Did you lose track of time? Now recall the activities that also gave you a feeling of positive feedback, that led to a feeling of something "clicking". What were those activities? Do you do them more or less frequently today? Do you wish you did them more?

Pick one of these activities that you put you "in the zone". Set aside a solid block of time to pursue this activity without distractions. Don't watch the clock, just focus on the activity. When your time is up or you feel you are satisfied, reflect back on the experience you had. Could you approach other activities in your life with a similar mindset?

Chapter Four:
Jobs, Creator

My goal wasn't to make a ton of money. It was to build good computers.

- Steve Wozniak

A lot of words have been used to describe Steve Jobs. Egomaniacal. Brilliant. Visionary. Stifling. Perfectionist. The stories around him are so familiar to most that they need not be repeated in this context. However, what does merit some exploration is how a small personal electronics maker became the most valuable company in the world to the tune of over half a trillion dollars in total, $200bn more than the next closest runner up.

What does this value even represent? If you sell 200 million widgets a year at $500 to $1,000 each, you are bound to make a fair amount of money. But is that really all there is to it? Apple is worth $300bn more than Exxon Mobile, nearly doubling the value of the largest oil and gas company in the world, a company that literally fuels the mechanical activity of the entire world. What resource, natural or otherwise, could Apple possibly be harnessing that makes them worth twice as much as the most successful purveyor of the most valuable natural resource in the history of the world? This mysterious resource at the core of Apple's valuation deserves closer inspection.

Like In-N-Out, Apple is aligned on a single purpose, sending a clear message to its customers: "You deserve this magical device." Furthermore, like Jiro, Jobs' obsession with perfection is well-documented. However, whereas Jiro relied on the signals in his customers' eyes, Jobs zeroed in on the vibrations within his heart as his primary source of feedback. In eschewing the direct feedback of his customers, Jobs took a Fosbury-like strategy to new heights. Commenting on this, Jobs famously stated that "it's really hard to design products by focus groups. A lot of times, people don't know what they want until you show it to them." Indeed, the secretive process of developing prototypes without consumer input continues to be a defining trait of Apple today.

During product development, Jobs made no secret as to when something was out of tune with this internal frequency. He observed every minute detail of the prototypes put before him. He was astutely knowledgeable about his competitors and the opportunities that they overlooked. He pushed his employees to iterate feverishly until something approaching his ideal was met.

Amidst this manic cycle, it may be difficult to identify a strong positive intent. However, amongst Jobs many industry-churning achievements, his greatest accomplishment was not tied to a specific device or service. His greatest achievement was in reminding the world that quality in design matters. For those that may be too young to remember, there was a time when computers were viewed as strictly utilitarian. Design, which can be a form of empathy for a user's experience, was previously viewed as a waste of capital.

Nobody cared what a computer looked like or how it felt as long as it worked. The result was generation after generation of grey, beige and black boxes. Jobs saw this trend and made it his life's work to reverse it.

Today, it seems odd to think of a consumer device without at least some degree of "fake hustle" exhibited in the design department. Given the central role these devices now play in our daily lives, it's not hard to imagine how much more banal our lives would be if no attention was ever paid to product design. The world is better off having been reawakened to the importance of quality work.

That said, is this $600bn worth of quality work? As important as quality is, a master woodcraftsman can also create unrivaled quality. What makes her work only worth a tiny fraction of what Apple produces?

To answer this, we need to go back to the words that are used to describe Steve Jobs. There is one word that is conspicuously missing.

Creative

Steve Jobs was creative. However, while creativity can be found in a variety of individuals, something else set Jobs and Apple apart: creative intent. Distinct from creativity, which can be a result of unconscious activities, creative intent is marked by a sense of purpose. Creative intent is applied creativity with the desire to actualize.

Could this be the missing driver of $600bn worth of value? Let's break it down. The iPhone itself is a product of world-class industrial design. But what is its single most important feature? Answer: the

App Store. One million plus apps have become deeply interwoven into how we live our daily lives. The best of these apps represent countless hours of applied observation, knowledge, iteration and positive intent. Their reach is unprecedented, spanning the globe while also settling into our living rooms and daily routines.

Steve Jobs was creative, yes. But above all else, he was the creator of a quality platform which in turn has allowed millions of other individuals to actualize their own creative intents, spawning their own billion dollar enterprises. It is this resource that Apple has harnessed in order to generate $600bn, i.e. capturing and channeling creative intent. And if there was ever a more definitive proof that focused creativity is the world's most valuable resource, look no further than the $300bn difference between Apple and Exxon Mobil.

However, here is the other thing about creative intent. Like any natural resource, unless it is nurtured and replenished, it can also be exhausted. Now that the app ecosystem has matured, the creative energy that it once inspired has begun to reach a plateau. In its place, a new impulse fills the void, the anti-matter to its matter.

Consumptive

When the iPhone was first created, it was a curiosity. It captured our imagination as to what was possible in a handheld device. Then, as millions of users adopted the iPhone as their daily driver for phone calls, internet access and music playback, it became a tool. Beyond that, as the concept of apps gained ground, the value of the iPhone multiplied a hundred-fold. It was not only a phone, but a streaming media device, a social media command center, a beacon for car services, a navigation device, a gaming device and so on and on.

As the initial burst of creativity founds its way into the lives of millions of users around the world, newfound relationships were established between high quality sources and their users. So valuable were these newfound relationships that several new billion dollar industries have blossomed from the app economy. The iPhone had become a platform.

Unfortunately, that is not where the story ends. We now find ourselves in another chapter. While the iPhone generated an initial burst of creativity from its developers and in turn a step change in productivity from its users, this initial explosion is beginning to wane.

As usage reaches a saturation point, smartphone growth will slow. For example, IDC research predicts that smart phone growth will slow to single digits by 2017 (down from nearly 40% year over year in 2013) (Dudau, 2014).

In addition to the maturation of the market, the profile of usage is also shifting as evidenced by the most popular apps today. 46 of the top 100 free apps in the app store are either games or intended for music/video consumption (iTunes Charts, 2015).

Finally, the evolution of the iPhone's impact may best be observed as we go about our daily lives; in lines at the coffee shop, waiting in the airport, wherever there is dead time, you will see the now familiar posture of smartphone consumption, i.e. phone up, head down.

Consumption and creativity are two stages of the same cycle just as inhaling and exhaling are two halves of the same breath. Consumption is a natural counterpart to creativity. However, when consumption of things, even those of high quality, becomes one's reason for living, it leaves no room for creativity, because, as with breathing, you simply can't inhale and exhale at the same time.

Gradually, insidiously, as more users look to the iPhone as a source of time-wasting diversions, the platform that Steve Jobs built becomes less a channel for creativity and more a channel for consumption. When this happens, the beautiful network effect at the core of the iPhone's app economy, where exceptional creative intent in turn inspires more creative impulses, will begin to slow and ultimately reverse.

With this reversal, Apple's most vital resource will begin to seep outside its control. This will not result in a fateful crash but it will be no less dangerous to Apple's future. To avoid this fate, Apple must refocus on what made it great, building platforms that inspire and empower others to realize their creative intents. The fact that even Apple, a product of a legendary creative force, can face this challenge at the apex of its success highlights the difficulty of sustaining this impulse. Long-term creative intent requires constant mindfulness and attention no matter whom you are or what you have achieved.

Every human activity, whether consciously performed or not, falls somewhere on the spectrum of being creative or consumptive. Similarly, forms found in nature are constantly built, broken, merged and transformed as well. However, there is a vital distinction between our actions and those found more broadly in nature: intent.

Humans uniquely share the ability to direct our intent towards one impulse or the other. Do you force yourself to sit down and write a short story or do you binge on Netflix? Do you practice your violin or do you snapchat for another hour? Indeed, the constant struggle between the instant gratification of consumption and long-term fulfillment of creativity is one of the most fundamental choices that makes us human. And the stakes have never been higher.

Over time, how each person approaches these minute to minute decisions informs where they fall on this continuum. This wavering balance, the constant interplay between creative and consumptive intent, is the fourth and final building block of the Improvement Axiom.

I am a firm believer that people are inherently creative. From a very early age, our minds begin to wander as to the possibilities, the what if's and the why's. Walk into any preschool in the world and you will see a wealth of imagination. Somewhere along the line, it's not that the creativity dies, but its intent gets dispersed or redirected towards unrewarding means.

Our problem isn't progression, it's location and direction. We move, but with no intent. We stand, but with no context. Today, if we are geographically lost, we look at our smartphones. If we are existentially lost, we are not so lucky. Fortunately, the Improvement Axiom can be both a compass and a map in this respect. So let's go ahead and build it.

Chapter Four Thought Exercises

Creative vs. Consumptive Intent.

On a scale of 1 to 10, 1 being highly consumptive and 10 being highly creative, how would you honestly rate yourself? Are you happy with this rating? Recall your answers from Chapter Three. If you did more of those activities, would you feel more creative as a result? What consumptive activities could you reduce to pursue more creative activities?

Set aside a block of time this week to do something creative. Anything. Paint, cook, write, sing, dance, build, etc. Be mindful of your own internal feedback as you create. Focus on this feedback more so than the result. Compare how you felt afterwards versus a typical consumptive activity, do you feel a difference?

Chapter Five:
The Axiom

The place to improve the world is first in one's own heart and head and hands.
- Robert Pirsig

We now have the four building blocks of the Improvement Axiom.

- First, Quality is a Relationship. It is not an intrinsic thing to be measured. Therefore, wherever there is a high quality signal then there is necessarily a high quality source.
- Second, the Black Box is the common thread between quality sources, the "recipe", the secret blend of eleven herbs and spices. This provides a roadmap for us to understand how both to assess high quality sources and, through time and effort, to replicate their strength and positivity.
- Third, a Sense of Resonance reveals that feedback need not be received solely in the context of crowds. Sometimes, the most valuable feedback is the kind felt within the vibrations of your core.
- Finally, Creative vs Consumptive Intent, perhaps the most important component for humanity. Nature can create

quality, it can create harmony, and it can even master the black box through evolution. However, one thing it cannot do is choose a direction. We can. And that is both empowering and frightening.

So how do we know what direction is better? With so many things vying for our attention, how do we cut through the noise? For that we need a filter and, thankfully, we have some building blocks at our disposal.

High Quality vs. Low Quality

First, let's differentiate between high and low quality. As we discussed in Chapter One, a high quality signal draws the source and receiver closer to each other. This can be a result of a deep-felt empathy for the receiver or, as discussed in Chapter Three, a well-tuned sensitivity to one's own internal feedback. In both cases, there is a search for clarity and connectedness.

High quality does not necessarily mean happy; it is primarily defined by this sense of connectedness. Take for example, a heartfelt song which moves you to tears. This feeling is not of happiness per se, but it is marked by authenticity, empathy and clarity, each of which helps the source and receiver relate to each other. In contrast, low quality signals typically lack either clarity or empathy. They are the "noise" in a signal to noise ratio. At best, they do not even register and, at worst, they repel the intended receiver. Having clarified the difference between high and low quality signals, let's place these as two poles of a mental map with high quality pointing North and low quality pointing South.

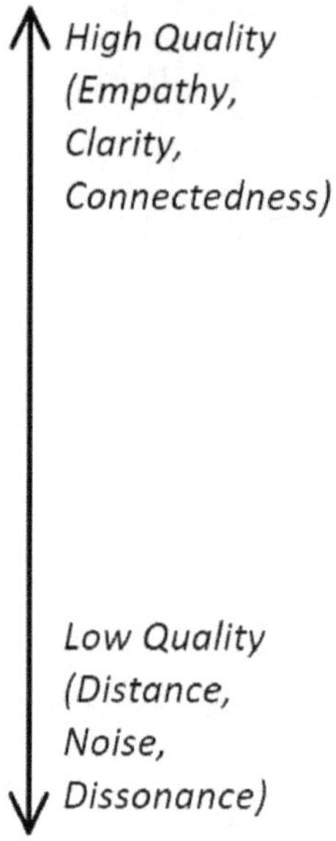

```
                    ↑ High Quality
                    │ (Empathy,
                    │ Clarity,
                    │ Connectedness)
                    │
                    │
                    │
                    │
                    │
                    │
                    │
                    │
                    │
                    │
                    │ Low Quality
                    │ (Distance,
                    │ Noise,
                    ↓ Dissonance)
```

Figure 1: North (High Quality) versus South (Low Quality)

Consumptive vs. Creative Intent

Secondly, let's differentiate between consumptive and creative intent. Understanding underlying intent is absolutely critical to understanding the long-term effects of one's activities.

To illustrate, take the primary activity in the world of business, i.e. growing a company's revenue. If the leaders of a business are building it with a creative intent in mind, i.e. creating a profitable enterprise that sends a strong and empathetic signal to its customers via its product and services, they are much more likely to keep their own incentives in line with both the company and its customers. However, if the leaders of the organization are consumptive in nature, i.e. looking to extract benefits from what they create over time, then the chances of their incentives staying in line with the best interests of the company and/or its customers are much much lower. Two similar companies, perhaps even two similar paths to start, but over time, the underlying intent and motivations of its leaders will ultimately reap two very disparate results.

Hypothetically, if the founders of In-N-Out had prioritized revenue growth above all else, trade-offs with respect to quality would inevitably have been made long ago. Freezing ingredients so they can be shipped longer distances? Ok. Streamlining and expediting employee training so more locations can be opened at a faster pace? Will do. Lowering the bar for hiring new location managers to further satisfy a demand for growth? Sure. As a matter of fact, there is probably a fast food business that has made exactly these tradeoffs within a stone's throw of your home. Thus, it is no mystery why In-N-Out has been able to maintain its level of quality while others have lowered that bar long ago in the name of expansion.

This is not to say that growth and quality are diametrically opposed. However, those companies that can expand while maintaining a quality relationship with their customers have undoubtedly invested their own creative energies into new processes and systems that specifically sustain those relationships. Without this degree of focus on maintaining a strong connection with its customers, a manager's decisions can have very real and very undesirable effects on the long-term trajectory of an organization.

Tools vs. Toys

It may be difficult to assess intent at first, but the easiest person to assess as a starting point is yourself. Which is not to say this is *easy*. With the noise we have to filter through on a daily basis, it's no wonder that sometimes we don't even really know why we do certain things. However, with practice, once you understand your own true intents for certain behaviors, you will begin to recognize similar motivations and symptoms within others.

Let's take an example. When you find yourself attracted to something, whether an object or activity, take a step back and ask yourself what impulse is this attraction speaking to? Is it satisfying a creative impulse or a consumptive impulse? Given the daily media assault we are subjected to in modern day society, it's no surprise that most impulses that we experience are consumptive in nature. Video Games. Cheesecake. Netflix. Even members of the opposite sex.

On the other hand, creative impulses are typically more subtle in nature and thus require a little more introspection to identify. For instance, as a gadget aficionado, I sometimes find it hard to figure out if I want a new piece of technology for creative purposes or because I just think it's really cool and would be fun to play with. A good rule of thumb I have developed for distinguishing creative impulses from consumptive impulses in this respect is to ask myself honestly whether it is a "tool" or a "toy". If the gadget in question will legitimately help me be more productive in my creative activities, e.g. a more versatile laptop that I can use to write on the go, then I can be more confident that it is a creative "tool". Sure, the laptop is cool as well but if I bought it with the mindset that it was largely something to watch movies on or play games on, then this would surely put it in the category of a consumptive "toy".

Although this analogy doesn't carry through perfectly to all other mediums, given how productized our lives currently are, the basic idea of tools vs toys generally holds up pretty well. Does this object or activity help to satisfy a short term need ("toy") or to build towards a longer term goal ("tool")? Is it for extracting short-term gratification or resources ("toy") or is it for the purpose of building a skill over time ("tool")? Just keep in mind, one person's tool may very well be another's toy. The same laptop I purchased with a creative intent in mind may very well be another person's game machine. Consequently, understanding a user's intent speaks far more about the utility of an object or activity than simplistic user ratings.

The Crystal Ball

As you go about your daily life, building an awareness of your own intents and impulses will prove invaluable in almost any pursuit you choose. Eventually, you will be able to identify these same impulses and intents in others and to place their activities and mindsets on a range of consumptive vs creative intent.

By identifying the underlying intents of others, it is almost like having a crystal ball that can peer into their mind. You will be able to anticipate what actions they take and intuitively understand what decisions they made for better or worse. In my own life, this has helped me to avoid, as best as I can, people who are highly consumptive in nature. This is not because they are bad people per se, just that I don't find spending time with those people particularly helpful for maintaining my own creative intents, especially within the context of my career. It is very true what they say, you are the company you keep.

Where I cannot avoid people with consumptive intents, I at least am armed with the knowledge of what motivates them and drives them. This cuts through any potential noise that may be created by false pretenses and allows me to focus on maintaining my own levels of creativity and quality.

Again, it's important to distinguish having consumptive intent from being "bad" or "evil". While in extreme cases, the outcomes may very well resemble something of this nature, I have found that most people fall somewhere within a more normalized range of behavior. In fact, by assessing whether someone is consumptive or creative rather than applying a label of an ethical or judgmental nature to them, it allows one to be more objective and empathetic with that person regardless of where they fall on the spectrum.

Empathy, as distinct from sympathy, doesn't mean you side with a person or support them, but simply that you can understand them and relate to them. In this regard, by sharpening your empathetic abilities, you are still in a much better position to engage effectively with people whether you agree with their motivations or not.

Let's take a concrete example, say a new sales person named Mary joined your company and within the first month happened to steal one of your key accounts, how should you assess this behavior? If you have come to judge Mary as someone who has a more consumptive-oriented intent, then chances are she stole this account without any particular goodwill. She was likely maximizing her own position so that she could continue to generate higher compensation and thus consume more material goods. Again, this isn't model behavior per se but it also isn't surprising once you understand her underlying intent.

If, on the other hand, you have assessed Mary as being a more creative-oriented individual who is more motivated by building a strong company and connecting with her customers, then it may be worth giving her the benefit of the doubt. In this case, you could plan to engage her more directly and speak openly about establishing account boundaries and proper sales protocols. These rules of engagement should make everyone more effective by providing clarity and consistent expectations going forward. If Mary is motivated by building a better company, these clear ground rules should appeal to her because they also protect her work from the misunderstandings of others.

There is also a third option whereby you feel you do not have enough information yet to assess Mary's intent. In this case, it still may be helpful to confront her directly. However, the objective would be slightly different. Rather than just setting protocols and clarifying behavioral expectations, you are also gauging her responses.

This is where a Sense of Resonance plays a huge part in our ability to read people's intents. Take into account what they say, their tone and their body language. If there are any inconsistencies in their behavior or rationale, this is also worth noting. Even if you ultimately have to sacrifice your key account, this fact-finding process should give you much better insight into Mary's intent. This assessment, in turn, will be extremely helpful if you ever have to confront her again down the road.

The Improvement Axiom

So now that we have clarified intent as well as some ways to identify it, let's put this range down as a horizontal axis within our framework with creative intent pointing East and consumptive intent pointing West.

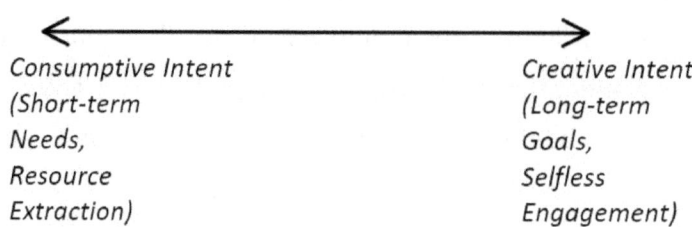

Consumptive Intent   Creative Intent
(Short-term   (Long-term
Needs,   Goals,
Resource   Selfless
Extraction)   Engagement)

Figure 2: East (Creative Intent) versus West (Consumptive Intent)

Now, we can combine these two axes to create a 2 x 2 matrix. Lay one over the other and you get the following mental map:

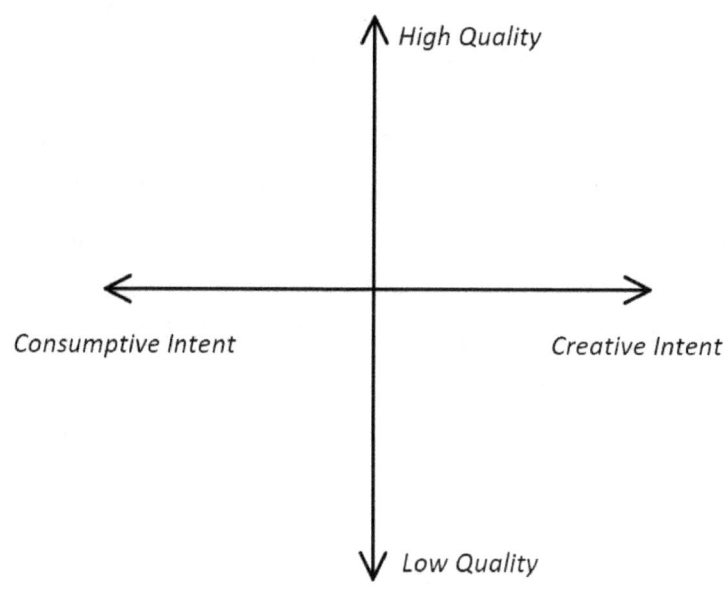

Figure 3: The Improvement Axiom

This is the map of the Improvement Axiom. North, South, East, West. A measure of signal quality vs a measure of intent. That's it. Simple to picture, but this map can capture the full range of the human experience. The point of intersection between the two axes separates this range into four equal quadrants. These are what we will explore next. As we step through each of these quadrants, we will explore some observable symptoms of spending time and energy in any given sector. Hopefully, as you build this mental map, you will be able to better diagnose yourself and begin the process of tuning your internal heart string. Here we go.

Lower Right - Low Quality & Creative Intent
"The Land of Fake Hustle"

First, lower right quadrant, low quality with creative intent or as I like to call it the "Land of Fake Hustle". When you are a creator of low quality signals, at best you go unnoticed and at worst you create distance. Whereas high quality signals generate a feeling of synchronicity, low quality signals create a feeling of discordance. Think of a lovingly home cooked meal versus a half-cooked hot dog by a preoccupied street vendor. This quadrant is characterized by action without intent. It is creative intent but lacking clarity and empathy. As a result, those who spend their energies in this sector may often feel like they are "going through the motions" or "moving in slow motion". In extreme cases, where a lack of empathy veers towards antagonism, connectedness is replaced by extreme distance. Over the long term, this can only lead to isolation of the individual and a feeling of emptiness.

Lower Left - Low Quality & Consumptive Intent
"The Land of Empty Calories"

Next, lower left quadrant, low quality with consumptive intent or the "Land of Empty Calories". Individuals who reside in this quadrant consume the equivalent of junk food for the soul. Spiritual Cheetos and mental Mac and Cheese. Dwelling in this quadrant is understandable as all empty calories have a similar trait, they taste really really good. So, activity in this sector is marked by instant gratification with little long-term benefit. However, the other trait of empty calories is they never satisfy you for very long. As a result, as the feeling of gratification wanes, the "hunger" for more consumption surfaces again. Not surprisingly, those who spend their energies in this sector may often feel a restlessness associated with this hunger and/or a general malaise resulting from a malnourished imagination.

Upper Left - High Quality & Consumptive Intent
"The Land of Conspicuous Consumption"

Upper left quadrant, high quality with consumptive intent or the "Land of Conspicuous Consumption". While consumption of high quality things in moderation is a natural counterpart to the creative process, consumption of high quality things in excess can be the most dangerous of the four quadrants.

We as a society tend to equate price with quality. We also tend to equate the quality of things with the people who can afford to buy them. Thus, while some individuals who spend time in this quadrant are truly looking for inspiration and connectedness, there are others who seek consumption of high quality things either to fill a vast hunger for instant gratification or to portray themselves as high quality people by consuming quality things rather than creating them. In this sense, the former are not too different from those who consume "empty calories". The latter, by associating their self-worth with material or transient things, will find themselves in a relentless and exhausting pursuit of "the next big thing". In either case, given the financial resources of some in this quadrant, this hunger runs the risk of growing to insatiable levels, leading these individuals to indulge on an endless feast of consumable goods and services.

Look in any tabloid and chances are you will find someone who dwells in this quadrant. Individuals in this quadrant may feel a hunger that grows in parallel with their resources to consume them, but their feelings of fulfillment will not. These individuals may occasionally consume truly high quality things amidst the other baubles, but any high quality signals contained within will likely fall on deaf ears.

High Quality & Creative Intent
"The Land of Little Victories"

Finally, the upper right quadrant, high quality with creative intent or the "Land of Little Victories". This is where the magic happens. But it is not effortless spellcasting as with the flick of a wand. This is magic as a craft; a master illusionist incrementally creating a spectacle so grand and so imaginative that it captures the world's imagination. When creative intent combines with the clarity and empathy of high quality work, then the individual in this sector has made the leap and begun to broadcast their signal into the world. It may be a weak signal at first but, if an individual is attentive enough, there is always feedback, both positive and negative, that can help strengthen the signal over time.

The hardest thing about this sector perhaps is simply staying in it. This is not an existence that thrives off of huge wins, it is a life of savoring the little victories. For those individuals who dwell in this space, they often have feelings of disappointment, surprise, joy, fear, suspense, enlightenment and, of course, fulfillment. Creators who build know the path is fraught with perils and may ultimately end in failure. However, even failure can be feedback, the world telling you that you need to retune and reboot but, oddly enough, you are still on the right track.

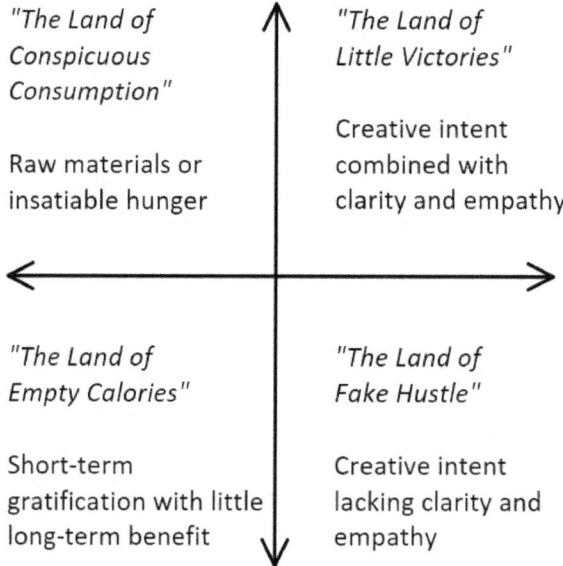

Figure 4: The Four Quadrants of the Improvement Axiom

Applying the Axiom

If you think of your own experiences and intent, how would you plot it? If you could imagine that for each meaningful experience you have had, you placed a single dot on the Axiom, what would it look like over time? Within which quadrant would it be weighted?

Granted, very few of us can spend 100% of our time in the "Land of Little Victories". As discussed prior, you can't create without some consumption. This would be the equivalent of only exhaling and never inhaling. However, what we can control is how our activity is weighted and where our intent is focused. This is the map with which we can constantly tune our experiences going forward. Observe something low quality either as a creator or consumer? Then learn why it occurred, what circumstances led you to that situation and then iterate away from those circumstances. This is the work required to move towards a specific direction. Intent combined with direction equals progress over time.

Everyone has to start somewhere so there is no shame in knowing where you stand at this point in time. That is observation in play. There are two clear paths that can lead you to creating little victories.

The first option is to think back to one dot that you placed in the upper right. Whatever it may have been, baking cookies, taking a photo, writing a long thoughtful email, playing a sport, dancing, anything. Think back to any situation where you felt like you had sent a high quality signal into the world or like you were creatively "in the zone". It doesn't matter if you were in a crowd or by yourself as we have established with the third building block.

A second option is to think back to a dot that you placed in the upper left where you felt inspired by a truly high quality signal. Was there ever something that resonated so deeply with you that you thought, "Wow, I wish I could do that?" Imagine yourself sending your own unique version of that high quality signal.

In either case, finding these activities or crafts that resonate with you are an essential ingredient to leading a higher quality life. Once you have identified some of these pursuits, set some time aside to invest in them. Remember, there will always be other things demanding your attention. Sometimes, the hardest thing to do when pursuing a higher quality life is to take the first step. If consumption wasn't so tempting, everyone would be busy creating high quality relationships already. Clearly not the case.

When you take that first step, be mindful of your own internal feedback. Is it frustrating at times? Is there something you feel like you can do better? Is there trial and error? Don't get too caught up in the dialogue but act as if you are an outside observer in your own mind, watching your own progress. Once you have completed your first session, take a step back and observe how you feel. Do you feel different than if you had taken that same time and allocated it to a consumptive activity?

If you did feel different and have more interest in pursuing this creative outlet then, congrats, you may have found your very own radio tower! The next step is to schedule some more time, ideally on a consistent basis in your life, either daily or every couple of days. Longer than a week and you risk losing focus or getting sidetracked by other demands.

Conversely, if you realized you don't have an interest in this particular activity then that is ok too! Just go back to the prior step and find another dot in the quadrant that might be worth trying.

Tuning Your Frequency

Once you have identified an activity or craft that you are interested in exploring over a longer term, try to refine your efforts by applying elements of the "black box". Observe, learn and iterate to tune your own radio tower. A brief review of those concepts can be found below:

Observe. How would it feel if you sent a similarly high quality signal? What would the positive feedback feel like? In what form might it take, i.e. from others or from yourself, expressed with body language or the written word, etc.? What would negative feedback feel like? What could you tweak or modify in response to negative feedback?

Learn. How could you send a stronger signal over time? Are there others you admire or know that have created a similarly strong signal using this medium? How did they get to that point over time? What techniques did they use that may be applicable to your situation? Who were their inspirations?

Iterate. Be methodical. Try different things. Take note of whether there was a stronger signal or weaker signal, whether the feedback was stronger or weaker. Massage the octopus for 15 more minutes. Take note of customer's eyes as they eat it. Try a different style, a different approach, a different angle. See what happens. This is the black box as it can be applied to your life.

Finally, what ultimately separates high quality creators from others is their positive intent. Signals are meant to be shared with others. Whatever you do, if you pursue excellence, it has the potential to inspire others. Keeping that in mind will give you that much more motivation to push forward even when you feel like you have hit a wall.

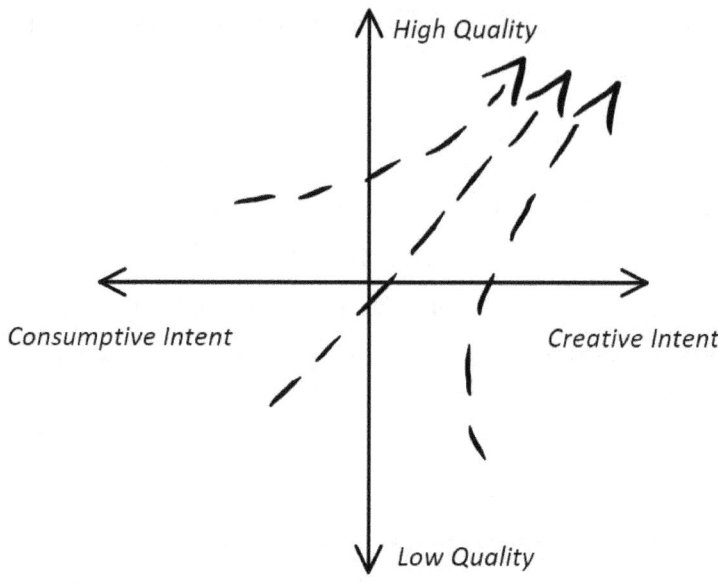

Figure 5: Iteration Towards the Upper Right

This is the Improvement Axiom. It is a simple two by two matrix which can be applied universally to all situations, constructs and decisions. Although it can be used to plot all of human experience, it has a singular direction which unifies long term benefit for the individual and the society in which he or she lives. I ask of you, if we all focused our intents on creating high quality experiences and sharing these with others, wouldn't our world and our lives be **better**?

Chapter Five Thought Exercises

The Improvement Axiom.

Try using the Axiom to mentally plot some of your daily experiences in real-time. If an ad catches your eye, consider what impulse it is speaking to. If a particular personal interaction stands out in your mind, try to assess whether that individual's intent is consumptive or creative in nature. Whatever experience resonates with you on some level, consider where you might plot it on your own matrix of intent vs. quality.

Like training a muscle, you will begin to feel greater levels of perception and mindfulness the more you practice this exercise. The insights drawn from these observations will, in turn, help to inform your decisions and actions as you iterate towards a higher quality life.

Part Two:

Essays

The following essays are a series of reflections on quality and creativity published on Medium and other publications. They attempt to apply the Improvement Axiom framework, either explicitly or implicitly, across various topics including the nature of good and evil, the fundamental discordance between hatred and religion and the role that excellence plays in America's increasingly segregated public school systems.

Chapter Six "What if the Opposite of Hitler... Was You" was in part a tongue-in-cheek response to a blogger's humorous exploration of an intentionally unanswerable question, "What is the Opposite of Hitler?" That said, I believe the essay also demonstrates the power of the Improvement Axiom to understand and identify the behaviors of even the most extreme individuals that humanity has encountered in history. The goal obviously is not to sympathize with Hitler but to understand what drove him to such destructive ends. What were his underlying intents? And if possible, whom could we identify that exhibits an equal and opposite level of intent?

Chapter Seven "The Selective Dissonance of Hateful Gods" was a response to ongoing wars and terrorist activities around the world that stem from religious fundamentalism. It speaks to a longstanding discordance between the positive traits that we typically associate with the concept of God, that of the Creator(s) and the Supreme Being(s), and the views of those who use violence in God's name. Again, in attempting to elucidate a very delicate and sensitive issue, the Improvement Axiom lays out why those who kill in God's name may feel perfectly in tune with their own concept of God while sowing such traumatic discordance with those around them.

Finally, Chapter Eight "A Question of Education and Excellence", was an op-ed originally printed in the *West Side Rag* in the upper west side of Manhattan. It is a response to a controversy surrounding two neighboring public elementary schools, i.e. PS 199 and PS 191, that has garnered national attention with coverage by the *New York Times*, the *NY Post* and *MSNBC*. These schools are on opposite sides of the spectrum in nearly every respect including ethnic demographics, socioeconomic disparity and a huge gap in academic performance. All this while being only nine blocks apart. In my published op-ed, I implicitly use the core principles of Quality as a Relationship both to empathize with parents that support maintaining the current system of de facto segregation and to make an argument for much-needed change.

As I publish more essays, I will seek to expand this section to include more content over time. However, if you would like to get immediate notification when a new essay is released, feel free to contact me via twitter at @theahchu or visit my medium page at www.medium.com/@theahchu to join my mailing list. In the meantime, I hope you find these essays thoughtful. I look forward to engaging in a continuing dialogue.

Chapter Six:

What if the Opposite of

Hitler... Was You?

(October 2015)

You brought music back into the house. I had forgotten.
- Captain von Trapp

The question was posed, what is the opposite of Hitler? (Sears, 2015)

Here's my shot.

In order to determine the opposite of Hitler, we must be able to place him on some vector with both a direction and a magnitude. Thereby, this would allow us to determine an opposite vector with an equal magnitude but opposite trajectory.

In order to determine this, we need some framework (ideally at least two-dimensional and not linear) that can objectively plot both Hitler's worst transgressions as well as the perceived opposite of those actions.

No easy task.

However, I would like to propose just such a framework (which I like to call the "Improvement Axiom") for your consideration and it looks like this:

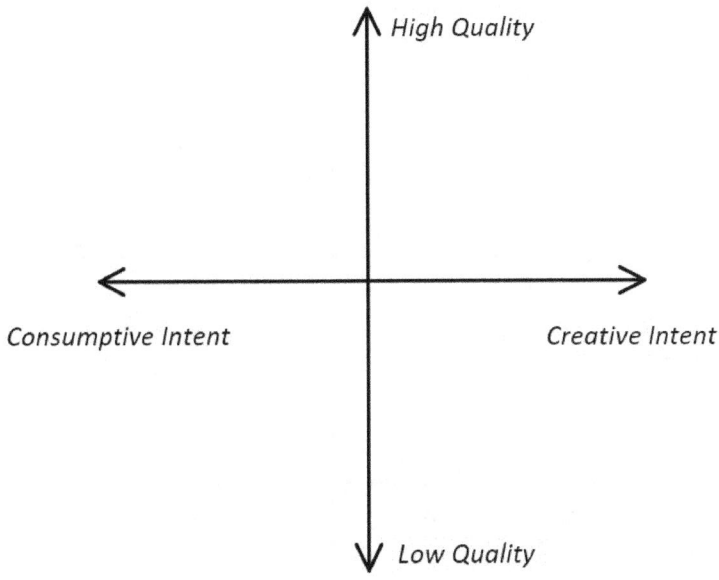

Two axes. One for quality vs. one for intent. That's it.

To clarify the definitions of quality and intent, please consider the following:

Something that is high quality resonates with you, it speaks to you. Conversely, something that is low quality repels you, it rings hollow.

Someone with creative intent focuses on building and sharing things, infusing herself into something larger. Conversely, someone with consumptive intent focuses on extracting things, elevating himself into something larger.

To lay this out in a more detailed manner, the axes would look as follows:

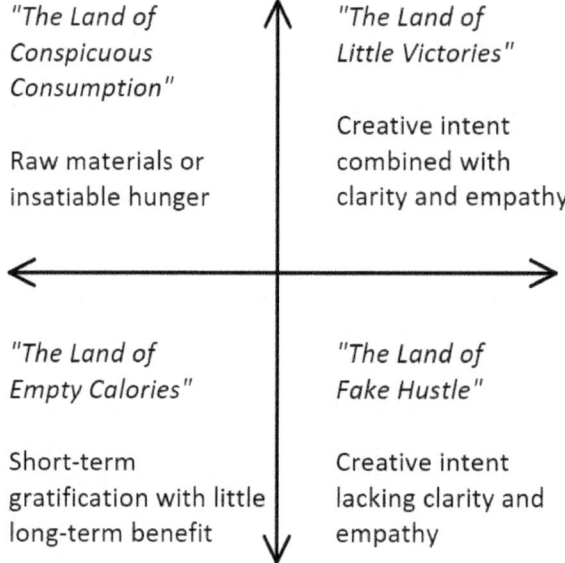

"The Land of Conspicuous Consumption"

Raw materials or insatiable hunger

"The Land of Little Victories"

Creative intent combined with clarity and empathy

"The Land of Empty Calories"

Short-term gratification with little long-term benefit

"The Land of Fake Hustle"

Creative intent lacking clarity and empathy

The strength of this framework is that it avoids the typical contradictions created by traditional measures of "good" or "bad" while still maintaining a high correlation with the individual's overall positive or negative long-term impact on society.

So does it work? Let's give it a shot and just tackle the big one. Hitler.

It would be rare to find anyone with a more consumptive mindset than Hitler. He consumed resources, souls and entire nations. That which he did not destroy in the process of consumption he then injected back into an ever-expanding system of political machinery which was diabolically designed to further expand his consumptive powers. This places him on the extreme far left of the matrix.

As far as quality, it is also difficult to imagine anyone who had a more dissonant effect on humanity. Hitler's modus operandi was to create extreme distance between himself and his foes, i.e. to destroy them, to wipe them off the face of the planet. Even his allies were maintained only to the extent that they helped him to expand his massive consumptive machinery.

So if one were to plot Hitler in the spectrum of human activity, he would go somewhere over here:

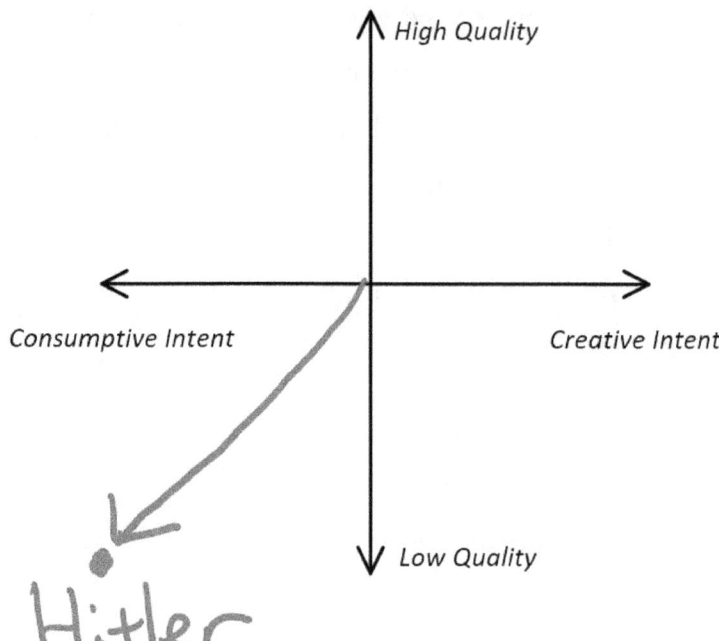

Conceptually, there aren't many more humans that would have such an extreme combination of those two variables. You would almost have to go to theoretical concepts to get further than him. Like, for instance:

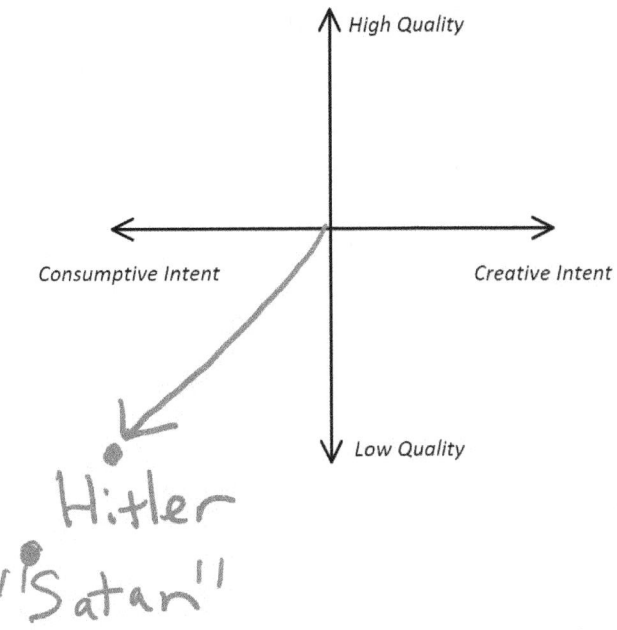

This is mostly in jest but it is also to make a point. Whereas traditionally the symbolic concept of "Satan" is perceived as all that is "evil" (which is a largely linear framework of good vs evil), within the Axiom framework "Satan" is objectively the theoretical extreme combination of consumptive intent and low quality. It just so happens that these two variables have almost a perfect correlation with what most of society (with perhaps the exception of Gilfoyle from *Silicon Valley*) views as evil.

Which leads us to the concept of opposites. We have explored the extremes of consumptive intent and low quality. What could have an equal magnitude but the exact opposite trajectory?

Whereas Hitler was concerned only with consumption, we need someone who is only concerned with creation. Whereas

Hitler was focused on creating extreme distance, we need someone who wanted to bring others closer together.

Ladies and gentlemen, I present to you, this woman as the Anti-Hitler.

The Real Maria Von Trapp. Courtesy: Wikipedia (Maria Von Trapp - Wikipedia, the free encyclopedia, 2015)

This is Maria Von Trapp. Yes, the real Maria, the one that wrote the memoir that inspired the German film that inspired the musical that inspired the movie that inspired the song that inspired millions of nursery room sing-a-longs since the movie Sound of Music was released in 1965.

Surprised? Perhaps you were expecting this Maria?

Maria #2. Inspiring, but not a real person.

Well, yes Julie Andrews' depiction of Maria was one for the ages and a huge reason why anyone knows the real Maria's story. However, Julie Andrews' Maria is not a real person. And Hitler was very very real.

So how could the real Maria Von Trapp, a woman who had no grand aspirations other than to sing with her family and live out her quiet life in Stowe, Vermont, how could she possibly be comparable in orders of magnitude to Hitler? If you plotted her on the chart, even with the benefit of the doubt, she might look something like this:

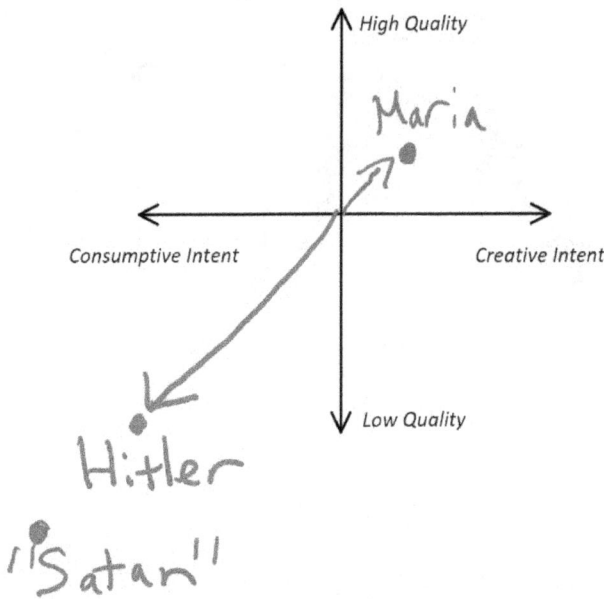

She clearly falls a bit short on her own. However, while she is perhaps more well-known by the works she inspired (of which she gained very little monetary compensation) than her own, her life was by no means insignificant for one crucial reason:

Without her living her life as she did, with courage, with humility and with creativity, we would have had none of the inspirational works that came after her.

No memoir. No German film. No musical. No movie. No Julie Andrews. No songs.

Just. An empty void.

From this:

Sadly, back to this:

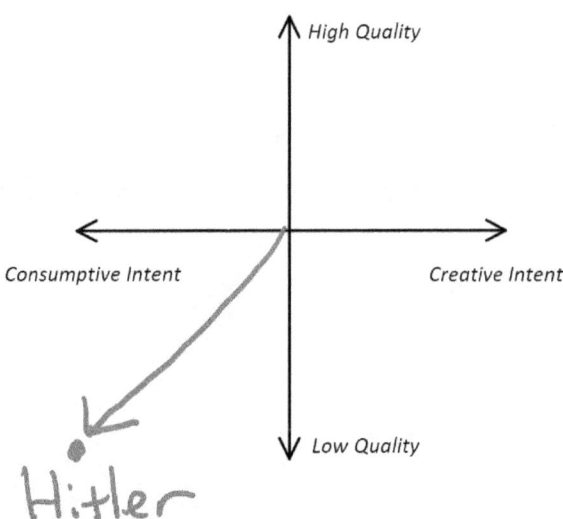

To be clear, Maria Von Trapp was no saint. In fact, contrary to the sunny disposition of Julie Andrews' Maria, she was described by her own children as having an unpredictable and fiery temper.

As her son, Johannes von Trapp, eloquently said in a New York Times article in 1998:

> *"[The] Sound of Music simplifies everything. I think perhaps reality is at the same time less glamorous but more interesting than the myth."*

The real Maria was certainly less glamorous than the fictional Maria. But here's the interesting thing about leading a high quality life with creative intent even if you aren't a Hollywood star:

Quality work inspires more quality work which inspires even more quality work... even if it isn't immediately observable at first.

That Maria chart? Let's look at it again, but this time let's follow the trail of inspiring works that came as a direct result of her life.

Yes, her legacy doesn't always travel in a straight line. Yes, the real Maria alone never had nearly the magnitude of impact that Hitler did on the world. All this is true. But in a way, isn't that even more encouraging?

In her way, in the way she lived, through the music she and her family created and through the sound of her voice, Maria Von Trapp was the Anti-Hitler.

But here's the thing. In our own ways, through our own music or powerpoints or handiwork or whatever craft we choose, we can all live the same way Maria did. We can all channel our creative intent through that which we create. In that way, we can all inspire a legacy of quality work that expands far beyond the reach of any one bad apple.

Together, we can all be Anti-Hitlers.

And one final thought, there is that one little dot remaining in the lower left. Is it ever possible to find the opposite of that?

We all have different things that resonate with us, that's the beauty of life. Sometimes, there are moments or creations that are of such high quality, that resonate so broadly that they can, in fact, change the world.

Reflecting on the climactic scene of the movie (spoiler alert!), the audience of the Salzberg Music Festival was so inspired by the Von Trapp's heartfelt ode to Austria that they summoned the courage to add their own voices, even amidst the watchful eyes of the tyrannical Nazi army.

Perhaps in a similar way, this movie and the songs it has etched into our collective memory has reached others deeply within their souls. Perhaps to another creator out there, brimming with both potential and uncertainty, the "Sound of Music" is more than just a movie. It's an idea, a symbol and a motivator that gives them hope for the future and a reason to live.

And without the real Maria living the way she did, that would have never come to pass. So thank you, Maria, for being the opposite of Hitler.

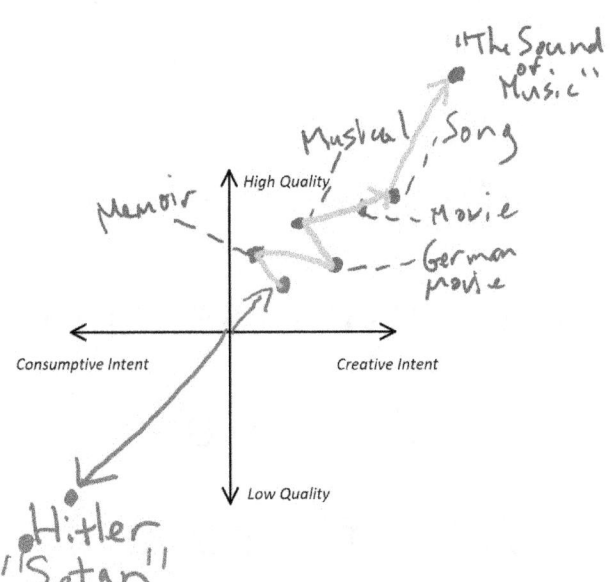

Chapter Seven:
The Selective Dissonance of Hateful Gods (November 2015)

Darkness cannot drive out darkness; only light can do that.
Hate cannot drive out hate; only love can do that.
- Dr. Martin Luther King Jr.

The Gods are fickle.

Why does it seem that religion can be used to justify most any view that us mortal beings hold?

How can these same views be vehemently defended by some and just as righteously opposed by others? Sometimes by individuals who by all rights actually share the same religion?

Is it truly the will of the Gods (whichever God you prescribe to) to sow these seeds of confusion and discord?

Or is something else going on?

In a prior article, I laid out the basic building blocks of what I refer to as the Improvement Axiom. It is a humble attempt to provide a simple but powerful roadmap for the human condition. It is depicted below:

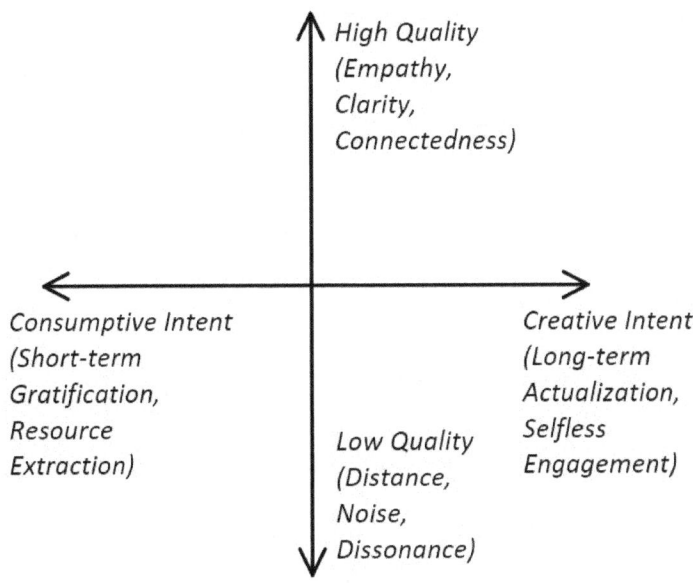

The Improvement Axiom

It consists of two axes, one a measure of quality, as defined by a feeling of connectedness or resonance, and the other a measure of creative vs consumptive intent. Combined, this framework can help organize a broad range of actions and events.

For example, if one were to ask what God represents, there are two identifiers that are broadly shared amongst most, if not all, of the world's religions: God as both the Creator and the Supreme Being(s).

God as the Creator.

Read another way, God is off-the-charts creative. Typically credited with creating the universe around us, God is, almost as a logical extension, as incomprehensible as the size and scale of the universe itself. In representing maximum theoretical creativity, our concept of God is a humble attempt to articulate a level of creative intent that, by definition, is more expansive than what human consciousness can grasp. Thus, God represents the theoretical and conceptual upper limit of creative intent.

God as the Supreme Being(s).

In other words, God is that which supersedes all else. As a concept, God underlies all that exists and all that occurs, encompassing and driving a vast network of invisible threads and forces. As innumerous as there are leaves on trees or blades of grass in the fields, this vast network of events and entities all draw their source from the concept of God. Again, God is our best effort to articulate the vastness and complexity of the forces around us and to make sense of all the possible relationships at play. Thus, God represents the theoretical and conceptual upper limit of connectedness or quality.

Thus, if one were to map the concept of God on the Improvement Axiom, for many who prescribe to the concept of God(s), it might look something like this:

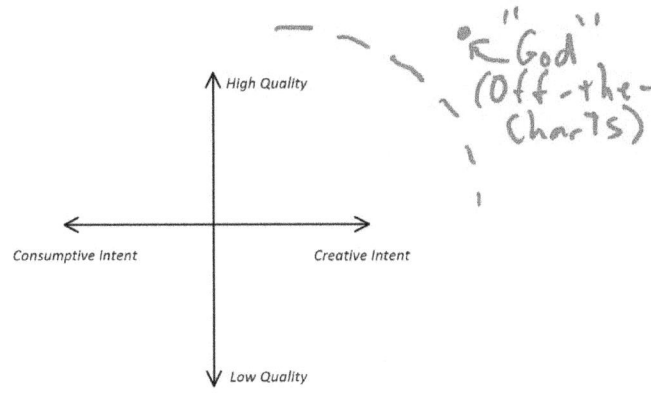

"God" is Off-the-Charts Creative and High Quality

So how does this explain the apparent fickleness of our Gods? What is driving these persistent issues of religious dissonance and discord that face humanity?

The key lies in that which we individually feel is resonant and creative.

For those that hold loathing, distaste or hatred in their hearts, then a hateful God would indeed be the most resonant with their desires. This concept of God "speaks" on a very fundamental level to those individuals who share a deep-seated detestation for a specific group or individual. Thus, in their mind, this is completely consistent with their worldview of what God should represent, i.e. a Supreme Being of the highest degree of connectedness.

In addition, for those that feel this resonance, it is also logical that they may spiritually, emotionally and, in some extreme cases, mortally commit themselves to what they feel is a greater cause. In their worldview, supporting the will of this God and creating an environment where this God can flourish is the highest creative intent possible.

Combine these two variables and one can begin to see why supporters of these hateful Gods see their Gods as off-the-charts Supreme and Creative.

In their mind, there is perfect congruency between the concept of God and their own condition.

But here is the fundamental issue. What hatred ultimately reaps is, in fact, the polar opposite of connectedness and creativity. In seeking to maximize their distance from the targets of their hatred either by isolation or by violence, the hateful are creating tangible rifts in the fabric of humanity. In seeking to strengthen their own condition by worsening the conditions of others, they, by definition, are consuming the resources, livelihoods and, in worst cases, the lives of others for their own gratification.

This is the source of the supreme dissonance created by Hateful Gods. Those who believe they stand apart from others may find supreme resonance with Hateful Gods but, in their isolation and selective segmentation of humanity, they, in actuality, are directly opposed to the true conceptual upper limits of quality and creativity.

As expansive as the universe is and as innumerous as the blades of grass are, true consistency with that which is a Supreme Creator would hold evident that all of humanity, including all of its imperfections, disparate conditions and differing worldviews, is captured within this universal concept of God.

It is on this basis, this fundamental truth, that Dr. Martin Luther King Jr. made his statement above. Hatred *severs*. Love *connects*.

Chapter Eight:
A Question of Education and Excellence
(November 2015)

*Only by being true to the full growth of all the individuals who
make it up, can society by any chance be true to itself*
- John Dewey

We are parents. And we have a very difficult question to answer.

The question is not what to do with PS199 or PS191. The question is not whether to move the lines or share the zone or, as proposed by myself and a small group of parents, to split by grades across now two and eventually three schools. The question is not even about diversity. While all of these questions are central to our children's futures, there is one question underlying them all. And that is, how do we define excellence in education?

As parents struggling to answer this question and all others that stem from it, we are all doing what we think is best for our children. And getting that right is extremely hard.

As parents trying to ensure a positive future for our children, we are constantly wrestling against all odds, despite the fact that not all of these odds are within our control. From putting rubber stoppers on corners of tables to choosing reputable schools with proven track records, we try as best we can to continuously shift these odds incrementally in our children's favor.

And why wouldn't we? It is only natural to want what's best for our children. It is only natural to want them to get into a good school, get good grades and get involved. It is only natural to want them to share the company of other families who share those very same goals.

But what if.

What if, in limiting the odds in our child's favor, we've somehow limited something else that is just as precious?

What if, in ensuring that our child goes to a good college, goes on to a good career and then goes on to something even better, we have overlooked something that is just as vital along the way?

What if, in pursuing our own definitions of education and excellence, we've shifted the odds too far?

Given what is at stake, coming to a definition of excellence that we are comfortable with is of an understandable degree of importance. It's also not an easy thing to determine.

Lacking any single, universal barometer of excellence, we, as parents, can only work with what we have, making leaps of logic and faith based on admittedly imperfect information. Having said that, there are some metrics that have seemingly gained broader acceptance than others. High test scores, national awards and even, regretfully, demographics are some typical metrics that we have taken on as proxies for excellence.

Without any more revealing data than what is available and lacking any better proxy to date, this seems to be the best definition a majority of us can agree upon.

But is this the best that we can do?

In assuming this definition, in shifting the odds so our children have the best chance of attending those institutions deemed excellent based on these limited measures, what are the potential risks?

If we assume an institution is excellent based on the aforementioned measures, is it then safe to assume an institution which is missing one or more of those measures is not? If we direct all our energies at preserving those institutions which have accumulated these metrics over time, do we risk isolating and abandoning those that have not? And perhaps, most critically of all, if we assume that the children within these institutions are capable of excellence, is it just to assume that children that are not within their walls are not equally capable of excellence?

Is it right to presume that, while a family may not have the means, the access or the prestige to attend such an institution, they are any less willing to achieve or any less likely to excel if given the proper resources to do so?

In pursuing a definition of excellence in education based on the qualities of the institution rather than the qualities of our children, does this best serve our children? Or the institution? For what is the true measure of excellence in education if not to reach out beyond our typical enclosures and nurture excellence in all its forms and variance?

If we accept this definition going forward, then, in the same way we shift the odds to protect our children, we incrementally shift the odds in favor of systems and processes and structures that protect this presumed definition of excellence at all costs.

But what, indeed, are the true costs of doing so?

What if, in shifting the odds to accommodate this presumed definition of excellence, we had excluded a representative segment of our district? What would be the risks involved with this separation? I believe the following quote from a teacher in

Hartford, CT most clearly describes the potential costs of doing so:

> "I think that children can overcome the stigma of poverty. I think children can overcome the stigma of their ethnicity. But what they cannot overcome is the stigma of separation. That is like a damned spot in their being, in their self-image. And that's what segregation does to children. They see themselves as apart and separate because of the language they speak, because of the color of their skin, the origin of their parents."

This is the cost. This is the collateral damage of collectively shifting the odds.

Is this a truly excellent outcome? Does this cost fit neatly within our presumed definition of excellence?

So what to do? Not an easy question or an easy answer.

But, perhaps, we can start with the uncomfortable process of introspection. Forget the rhetoric. Forget the camps, the titles, the roles. Just collectively and individually consider our own values, our own principles. What do we stand for? What do we strive for? Then perhaps, after this reflection, we, as a community, can make a decision as to how we *choose* to define excellence in education.

Alternatively, we can continue to methodically shift the odds in favor of certain institutions that exhibit these traits, and, over time, naturally limit access to those very same institutions as they become more and more taxed.

If given a choice, would you accept this definition and this outcome?

It is my sincere hope that my son enters a school system which not only tolerates diversity, and the naturally varied discourse that comes with that, but wholly embraces it as an integral part of its own definition of excellence.

I have hope that the New York City Public School System, rather than being the most segregated in the country, could instead be the most transformative.

The hard work put forth by a small group of parents from within our community was never intended to force a proposal upon others, but rather to present it as an option and a choice. This option, in summary, is as follows:

Starting in 2017, all incoming Kindergarten students currently zoned for either PS199 or PS191 would enroll at PS191 (or an incubated PS342) as a zone-wide "Super Class". These students would have a crucial opportunity, over the next 3 years, to grow together as a community prior to moving to PS199 for grades 3–5. For parents with current students at PS199 or PS191, your child would graduate from their current school with zero disruption. For parents with younger siblings about to attend PS199, sections could be formed specifically for siblings at PS199 to maintain continuity. These "Sibling Sections" would reunite with the larger "Super Class" when they all enter grade 3 at PS199.

Admittedly, for this choice to work, it would necessarily take all of us to commit, because, without the collective support of the community as a whole, any such decision of this magnitude would inevitably be met with strife and discontent. However, I must believe that applying our collective energies towards realizing this solution must be more favorable than the trauma and discord resulting from our current battles.

So an option and a choice has been presented which could potentially resolve multiple concurrent issues. By distributing demand across PS199, PS191 and, eventually, PS342, this proposal could immediately address overcrowding at PS199. By increasing seat utilization at PS191, it could guarantee all children a spot in Kindergarten rather than subject them to the 50/50 odds of a waitlist or lottery. By directly addressing the perception of "winners and losers" with the elimination of zone lines altogether, it avoids the heartache and trauma of future rezoning processes. By allocating our students based on grades rather than class, color or geography, it could take a small but momentous step towards reversing decades of de facto segregation. It could achieve all of these and, what's more, depending on the definition of excellence that you prescribe to, even provide a more excellent education than what some of us are grateful to have today.

However, in the end, after this option and this choice has been presented and duly considered by all stakeholders, it is then at the discretion of the community itself to determine our path forward. If we collectively decide this choice, this more expansive definition of excellence, and all the potent possibilities that it brings, is not for us and that we, instead, prefer the status quo, then, ultimately, we have no one else, absolutely no one else to blame, not the DOE, not the CEC, not 191, not 199, not each other.

We have no one else to blame for the impact this decision will have on our children but ourselves.

Afterword

First of all, thank you so much for taking the time to read this work. I really hope it will be helpful for whatever high quality endeavor you ultimately choose to pursue. I also would like to invite you to join me in an ongoing dialogue as this work evolves. I see this book as a living document and plan to add to it over time. However, in order to so, I would really like to hear feedback, both questions and comments, from you, the reader. So please take the time to leave a review and feel free to ask questions within your review.

In addition, I would like to offer my thanks to my friends and family whom, over the course of my life, have left strong impressions of quality and creativity in their own unique ways. I am truly blessed to have been given the opportunity to learn what makes a quality life firsthand from those closest to me.

References

Anderson, S. (2010, December 8). *$6.7 Billion Spent On Marketing Research Each Year*. Retrieved from MDX Research: http://www.mdxresearch.com/6-7-billion-spent-on-marketing-research-each-year/

Deaton, D. K. (2010). High income improves evaluation of life but not emotional well-being. *PNAS*, 1-5.

Dudau, V. (2014, February 27). *IDC: Smartphone annual growth to hit single digits by 2017; Windows Phone well equipped for the future*. Retrieved from Neowin: http://www.neowin.net/news/idc-smartphone-annual-growth-to-hit-single-digits-by-2017-windows-phone-well-equipped-for-the-future

Ebert, R. (2012, April 4). *Jiro Dreams of Sushi Movie Review (2012) | Roger Ebert*. Retrieved from rogerebert.com: http://www.rogerebert.com/reviews/jiro-dreams-of-sushi-2012

Fosbury Flop - Wikipedia, the free encyclopedia. (2015, March 6). Retrieved from Wikipedia: https://en.wikipedia.org/wiki/Fosbury_Flop

In-N-Out Burger - Wikipedia, the free encyclopedia. (2015, September 26). Retrieved from Wikipedia: https://en.wikipedia.org/wiki/In-N-Out_Burger

iTunes Charts. (2015, September 27). Retrieved from apple.com: http://www.apple.com/itunes/charts/free-apps/

Maria Von Trapp - Wikipedia, the free encyclopedia. (2015, November 17). Retrieved from Wikipedia: https://en.wikipedia.org/wiki/Maria_von_Trapp

Peper, G. (1987, September). Ben Hogan: The Golf Magazine Interview. *Golf Magazine*.

Pirsig, R. (1974, 1999). *Zen and the Art of Motorcycle Maintenance*. New York: HarperCollins e-books.

Posnanski, J. (2013, June 10). *Story behind photo of Hogan's 1-iron shot at Merion*. Retrieved from golfchannel.com: http://www.golfchannel.com/news/joe-posnanski/story-behind-photo-hogans-1-iron-shot-merion/

Sears, T. (2015, October 8). *The Opposite of Hitler*. Retrieved from Medium: https://medium.com/keep-learning-keep-growing/the-opposite-of-hitler-5eb570346020#.v6pjilyiy

www.ingramcontent.com/pod-product-compliance
Lightning Source LLC
Chambersburg PA
CBHW051219170526
45166CB00005B/1962